D0041553

Risking Everything

ALSO BY ROGER HOUSDEN

Dancing with Joy: 99 Poems (editor)

Seven Sins for a Life Worth Living

*How Rembrandt Reveals Your Beautiful, Imperfect Self:
Life Lessons from the Master*

Ten Poems to Last a Lifetime

Ten Poems to Set You Free

Ten Poems to Open Your Heart

Chasing Rumi: A Fable About Finding the Heart's True Desire

Ten Poems to Change Your Life

RISKING EVERYTHING

110 POEMS OF LOVE AND REVELATION

EDITED BY ROGER HOUSDEN

HARMONY BOOKS

NEW YORK

Copyright © 2003 by Roger Housden

All rights reserved. No part of this book may be reproduced or transmitted in any form or by any means, electronic or mechanical, including photocopying, recording, or by any information storage and retrieval system, without permission in writing from the publisher.

Published by Harmony Books, New York, New York.
Member of the Crown Publishing Group, a division of Random House, Inc.

www.randomhouse.com

Harmony Books is a registered trademark and the Harmony Books colophon is a trademark of Random House, Inc.

A complete list of credits for previously published material appears at the end of the book.

Printed in the United States of America

Design by Monica Elias

Library of Congress Cataloging-in-Publication Data

Risking everything : 110 poems of love and revelation / edited by Roger Housden.
1. Poetry—Collections. 2. Poetry—Translations into English. I. Housden, Roger.
PN6101 .R555 2003
808.81—dc21
2002014410

ISBN 1-4000-4799-4

20 19 18 17 16 15

CONTENTS

RISKING EVERYTHING

Introduction

Listen, are you breathing just a little, and calling it a life?
　　　　　　　　　　　　　　　　　　—Mary Oliver[1]

Have you ever longed for a life in which every last part of you is entirely used up? Have you ever followed that longing? Taken a step back from the known in your life and found yourself falling, falling, yet with the irrational certainty that the world is more right with you than it has ever been? Or dared to take a step forward and down into the known and humdrum details of your daily existence and suddenly found there a fullness of love and meaning as rich in its own way as others may know only through wild adventures?

　　The poems in this book call us to take that step. They can send us tumbling out of our familiar world—backwards or forwards, it doesn't matter—down into unknown landscapes where we may find a new life we never dreamed we were worthy of. Poetry has that power. It has it because it pours from those same depths. Look what it did to Pablo Neruda:

and something started in my soul,
fever or forgotten wings,
and I made my own way,
deciphering
that fire
and I wrote the first faint line,
faint, without substance, pure
nonsense,
pure wisdom
of someone who knows nothing,
and suddenly I saw
the heavens
unfastened
and open. . . .[2]

In their different ways, all the poems in this book reveal the
"Soul *at the White Heat*."[3] Some of them offer encouragement
for those of us who feel at times, or even often, that our life is
passing us by; that "the White Heat" is for the likes of Emily
Dickinson, not for ordinary people like us. Take any poem in
this book by Mary Oliver, and you will find a challenge to that
kind of misconception.

When it's over, I want to say: all my life
I was a bride married to amazement. . .

When it's over, I don't want to wonder
if I have made of my life something particular, and real.
I don't want to find myself sighing and frightened,
or full of argument.

I don't want to end up simply having visited this world.[4]

Feel the quiet intensity of Jane Hirshfield's words in her poem, "Lake and Maple":

> I want to give myself
> utterly
> as this maple
> that burned and burned
> for three days without stinting
> and then in two more
> dropped off every leaf; . . .[5]

There is, I believe, a longing in many of us, often unrequited, to give ourselves utterly to our lives, whatever that may mean to us individually. It's simple, perhaps, but not easy. I have known that heat, that falling in; but I know, too, those gray, restless days when life seems just to limp along. For all the beauty and love I have known, and still know, I sometimes wake up "empty and frightened."[6] Even though I love what I do, I still have the feeling at times that I should be making a fortune somewhere in the business of the moment in London or Manhattan, rather than writing books about poetry, love, and revelation in a hut in the woods of upstate New York. I would make a great magazine editor, too, but the people at Condé Nast don't seem to know that. This is one of the cracks in my world—the occasional but persistent idea that there is surely something more real, more resonant of life's marrow, to be found in some other pasture.

Yet it is precisely the crack in our lives that can let the light pour through. We do not spring into life perfectly formed. We each have our fault lines, and it is not by turning away from them that life suddenly takes on its full glory. No, I believe that we come to our fullness not in spite of our darkness, but in the embrace of it. That is why there are several poems in this anthology of "poems of love and revelation" whose subjects are loss, death, darkness, and failure.

And I said to myself:

"What have you done with the garden entrusted to you?"[7]

says the figure in one of Antonio Machado's poems. Not self-accusingly, but with a heart that, to use that beautiful old Christian term, feels shriven. The person who is speaking in the poem realizes that all the flowers in his garden are dead. He dares to look at the reality of his situation, and he is chastened. From that disillusionment, that paring away of what hides the truth, new life may spring.

The only true prayer, says Rumi, is an egg.

Hatch out the total helplessness inside.[8]

And a little earlier in the same poem, he urges us to pray the prayer that has no equal:

I have no hope. I am torn to shreds. You are my first and last and only refuge.[9]

We can only travel down through the truth of our lives on our own. Yet there is consolation, perhaps, in knowing that we are all on this journey together. It's all right, Robert Bly says,

There are more like us. All over the world
There are confused people, who can't remember
The name of their dog when they wake up, and people

Who love God but can't remember where

He was when they went to sleep. It's
All right. The world cleanses itself this way.[10]

Notice that last line—there is more than mere consolation in knowing that there is a purpose in all this apparently meaningless suffering. Not some grand purpose that we are all working our way toward; not suffering's glorification (it will always stink), but purpose in the sense that it is obviously part of what happens here. Seen this way, it is not personal. Suffering is part of how it is on earth; it is an inherent part of the fabric of existence. And if we are lucky, it will break our heart open. That is the crack that lets the light pour through. That is the way the world cleanses itself.

Not only that: our failures, our losses, our sufferings of all kinds, are inextricably woven into everything else—into the flowers, the sunrise, the great achievements of mankind, and into our own successes, too. It is all one great, swirling, unending, creation, and every last drop of our life, its darkness as well as its light, has its part to play. With a cast of mind that sees the shadows as part of our story, instead of something we need to be rid of, the world can look and feel different. That's what I love about another of Machado's poems, in which he says

> Last night, as I was sleeping,
> I dreamt—marvellous error!—
> that I had a beehive
> here inside my heart.
> And the golden bees
> were making white combs

110 POEMS OF LOVE AND REVELATION

and sweet honey
from my old failures.[11]

That's the way it is in this world:

one moment your life is a stone in you, and the next, a star.[12]

As some of these poems will show you, the way to the star can often be to pick up the stone. Then there are those moments, hours, even days of pure grace, utter happiness that for no reason at all can burst in on our lives and fill our hearts with love, with gratitude, and can open our eyes to an entirely fresh way of seeing the world. You know how it is: you look up from weeding the garden, and there, barely a yard or two away, is a thrush on a branch, head cocked your way, glassy eye on you. And you waken into the world. Or you are driving, as Seamus Heaney was one day, and the light and the wildness around you suddenly "catch the heart off guard and blow it open."[13] Neruda's "Ode to My Socks," Levertov's "O Taste and See," Kinnell's "Oatmeal," Lawrence's "Snake"—there are many poems here that capture such moments of revelation—for how else would you name them?

There are many, too, that speak of the degrees of love. And love itself is always a revelation, swooping down as it does from branches we never knew were there. We fall into love, too, and always backwards, for we never know where love is taking us. Our sober grip on reality is shaken loose and we are delivered up into love's full flare. That's what Nikki Giovanni's wonderful poem "I Take Master Card" would have us do: throw all caution to the wind and charge love's credit card to the full.

Look at any poem by Anna Swir in this collection, and you will find that same abandonment to joy.

Robert Bly, in his poem "The Third Body," summons a quieter love, the presence that can emerge between people when they are at rest in themselves. There are poems here, too, which rise from a deep well of compassion, and convey a love not only for one person, but also for those whose suffering draws out our own tenderness. I am thinking of Naomi Shihab Nye's poem "Kindness"; but also of Galway Kinnell's "Parkinson's Disease" and Dorianne Laux's "For the Sake of Strangers." And finally, there is the love that is not of this world; the love of Mirabai, Hafiz, or Rumi—men and women who have fallen through the concerns of this life to live in the invisible fire in the heart of hearts.

The poems in this anthology are drawn from all over the world, and from every era of history. How could it be otherwise, since there is no time or place where love and revelation have not informed and inspired human existence? Taken together, they represent a great song of what is possible for us—all the ways in which a life can be fully lived. And the risk? The risk they urge us toward is the forgetting of our familiar lamentations for a moment and the taking of that tiny yet momentous step—the willingness to try on the life that is truly ours. Derek Walcott says it this way in these few lines from his poem "Love After Love":

Take down the love letters from the bookshelf,

The photographs, the desperate notes,
Peel your image from the mirror.
Sit. Feast on your life."[14]

That is the simplest way, to let the poems speak for themselves. Better to turn the page, and fall in!

NOTES

1. From "Have You Ever Tried to Enter the Long Branches" by Mary Oliver
2. From "Poetry," by Pablo Neruda
3. From "Soul *at the White Heat*" by Emily Dickinson
4. From "When Death Comes" by Mary Oliver
5. From "Lake and Maple" by Jane Hirshfield
6. From "Today Like Every Other Day" by Rumi, translated by Coleman Barks
7. From "The Wind, One Brilliant Day" by Antonio Machado, translated by Robert Bly
8. From "Prayer Is an Egg" by Rumi, translated by Coleman Barks
9. Ibid.
10. From "People Like Us" by Robert Bly
11. From "Last Night As I Was Sleeping" by Antonio Machado, translated by Robert Bly
12. From "Sunset" by Rainer Maria Rilke
13. From "Postscript" by Seamus Heaney
14. From "Love After Love" by Derek Walcott

Risking Everything

WHEN DEATH COMES

Mary Oliver

When death comes
like the hungry bear in autumn;
when death comes and takes all the bright coins from his purse

to buy me, and snaps the purse shut;
when death comes
like the measle-pox;

when death comes
like an iceberg between the shoulder blades,

I want to step through the door full of curiosity, wondering:
what is it going to be like, that cottage of darkness?

And therefore I look upon everything
as a brotherhood and a sisterhood,
and I look upon time as no more than an idea,
and I consider eternity as another possibility,

and I think of each life as a flower, as common
as a field daisy, and as singular,

and each name a comfortable music in the mouth,
tending, as all music does, toward silence,

and each body a lion of courage, and something
precious to the earth.

When its over, I want to say: all my life
I was a bride married to amazement.
I was the bridegroom, taking the world into my arms.

When it's over, I don't want to wonder
if I have made of my life something particular, and real.
I don't want to find myself sighing and frightened,
or full of argument.

I don't want to end up simply having visited this world.

LOVE AFTER LOVE

Derek Walcott

The time will come
When, with elation,
You will greet yourself arriving
At your own door, in your own mirror,
And each will smile at the other's welcome,

And say, sit here, Eat.
You will love again the stranger who was your self.
Give wine. Give bread. Give back your heart
To itself, to the stranger who has loved you

All your life, whom you ignored
For another, who knows you by heart.
Take down the love letters from the bookshelf,

The photographs, the desperate notes,
Peel your image from the mirror.
Sit. Feast on your life.

WILD GEESE

Mary Oliver

You do not have to be good.
You do not have to walk on your knees
for a hundred miles through the desert, repenting.
You only have to let the soft animal of your body
    love what it loves.
Tell me about despair, yours, and I will tell you mine.
Meanwhile the world goes on.
Meanwhile the sun and the clear pebbles of the rain
are moving across the landscapes,
over the prairies and the deep trees,
the mountains and the rivers.
Meanwhile the wild geese, high in the clean blue air,
are heading home again.
Whoever you are, no matter how lonely,
the world offers itself to your imagination,
calls to you like the wild geese, harsh and exciting—
over and over announcing your place
in the family of things.

TODAY I WAS HAPPY, SO I MADE THIS POEM

James Wright

As the plump squirrel scampers
Across the roof of the corncrib,
The moon suddenly stands up in the darkness,
And I see that it is impossible to die.
Each moment of time is a mountain.
An eagle rejoices in the oak trees of heaven,
Crying
This is what I wanted.

POETRY
Pablo Neruda

And it was at that age . . . Poetry arrived
in search of me. I don't know, I don't know where
it came from, from winter or a river.
I don't know how or when,
no, they were not voices, they were not
words, nor silence,
but from a street I was summoned,
from the branches of night,
abruptly from the others,
among violent fires
or returning alone,
there I was without a face
and it touched me.

I did not know what to say, my mouth
had no way
with names
my eyes were blind,
and something started in my soul,
fever or forgotten wings,
and I made my own way,
deciphering
that fire,
and I wrote the first faint line,
faint, without substance, pure
nonsense,
pure wisdom
of someone who knows nothing,
and suddenly I saw

the heavens
unfastened
and open,
planets,
palpitating plantations,
shadow perforated,
riddled
with arrows, fire and flowers,
the winding night, the universe.

And I, infinitesimal being,
drunk with the great starry
void,
likeness, image of
mystery,
felt myself a pure part
of the abyss,
I wheeled with the stars,
my heart broke loose on the wind.

—Translated by Alastair Reid

THE GATE

Marie Howe

I had no idea that the gate I would step through
to finally enter this world

would be the space my brother's body made. He was
a little taller than me: a young man

but grown, himself by then,
done at twenty-eight, having folded every sheet,

rinsed every glass he would ever rinse under the cold
and running water.

This is what you have been waiting for, he used to say to me.
And I'd say, What?

And he'd say, This—holding up my cheese and mustard
    sandwich.
And I'd say, What?

And he'd say, This, sort of looking around.

SHOVELING SNOW WITH BUDDHA

Billy Collins

In the usual iconography of the temple or the local Wok
you would never see him doing such a thing,
tossing the dry snow over the mountain
of his bare, round shoulder,
his hair tied in a knot,
a model of concentration.

Sitting is more his speed, if that is the word
for what he does, or does not do.

Even the season is wrong for him.
In all his manifestations, is it not warm and slightly humid?
Is this not implied by his serene expression,
that smile so wide it wraps itself around the waist of the
    universe?

But here we are, working our way down the driveway,
one shovelful at a time.
We toss the light powder into the clear air.
We feel the cold mist on our faces.
And with every heave we disappear
and become lost to each other
in these sudden clouds of our own making,
these fountain-bursts of snow.

This is so much better than a sermon in church,
I say out loud, but Buddha keeps on shoveling.
This is the true religion, the religion of snow,

and sunlight and winter geese barking in the sky,
I say, but he is too busy to hear me.

He has thrown himself into shoveling snow
as if it were the purpose of existence,
as if the sign of a perfect life were a clear driveway
you could back the car down easily
and drive off into the vanities of the world
with a broken heater fan and a song on the radio.

All morning long we work side by side,
me with my commentary
and he inside the generous pocket of his silence,
until the hour is nearly noon
and the snow is piled high all around us;
then, I hear him speak.

After this, he asks,
can we go inside and play cards?

Certainly, I reply, and I will heat some milk
and bring cups of hot chocolate to the table
while you shuffle the deck,
and our boots stand dripping by the door.

Aaah, says the Buddha, lifting his eyes
and leaning for a moment on his shovel
before he drives the thin blade again
deep into the glittering white snow.

WE SHALL NOT CEASE
(FROM LITTLE GIDDING)

T. S. Eliot

We shall not cease from exploration
And the end of all our exploring
Will be to arrive where we started
And know the place for the first time.
Through the unknown, remembered gate
When the last of earth left to discover
Is that which was the beginning;
At the source of the longest river
The voice of the hidden waterfall
And the children in the apple-tree
Not known, because not looked for
But heard, half-heard, in the stillness
Between two waves of the sea.
Quick now, here, now, always—
A condition of complete simplicity
(Costing not less than everything)
And all shall be well and
All manner of thing shall be well
When the tongues of flame are in-folded
Into the crowned knot of fire
And the fire and the rose are one.

On Angels

Czeslaw Milosz

All was taken away from you: white dresses,
wings, even existence.
Yet I believe you,
messengers.

There, where the world is turned inside out,
a heavy fabric embroidered with stars and beasts,
you stroll, inspecting the trustworthy seams.

Short is your stay here:
now and then at a matinal hour, if the sky is clear,
in a melody repeated by a bird,
or in the smell of apples at the close of day
when the light makes the orchards magic.

They say somebody has invented you
but to me this does not sound convincing
for humans invented themselves as well.

The voice—no doubt it is a valid proof,
as it can belong only to radiant creatures,
weightless and winged (after all, why not?),
girdled with the lightning.

I have heard that voice many a time when asleep
and, what is strange, I understood more or less
an order or an appeal in an unearthly tongue:
day draws near
another one
do what you can.

Holy Spirit

Hildegard of Bingen

Holy Spirit,
giving life to all life,
moving all creatures,
root of all things,
washing them clean,
wiping out their mistakes,
healing their wounds,
you are our true life,
luminous, wonderful,
awakening the heart
from its ancient sleep.

—Translated by Stephen Mitchell

PEOPLE LIKE US

Robert Bly

for James Wright

There are more like us. All over the world
There are confused people, who can't remember
The name of their dog when they wake up, and
   people
Who love God but can't remember where

He was when they went to sleep. It's
All right. The world cleanses itself this way.
A wrong number occurs to you in the middle
Of the night, you dial it, it rings just in time

To save the house. And the second-story man
Gets the wrong address, where the insomniac lives,
And he's lonely, and they talk, and the thief
Goes back to college. Even in graduate school,

You can wander into the wrong classroom,
And hear great poems lovingly spoken
By the wrong professor. And you find your soul,
And greatness has a defender, and even in death
   you're safe.

My Dead Friends

Marie Howe

I have begun,
when I'm weary and can't decide an answer to a bewildering
   question

to ask my dead friends for their opinion
and the answer is often immediate and clear.

Should I take the job? Move to the city? Should I try to conceive
   a child
in my middle age?

They stand in unison shaking their heads and smiling—
   whatever leads
to joy, they always answer,

to more life and less worry. I look into the vase where Billy's
   ashes were—
it's green in there, a green vase,

and I ask Billy if I should return the difficult phone call, and
   he says, yes.
Billy's already gone through the frightening door,

whatever he says I'll do.

TODAY, LIKE EVERY OTHER DAY
Rumi

Today, like every other day, we wake up empty
and frightened. Don't open the door to the study
and begin reading. Take down a musical instrument.

Let the beauty we love be what we do.
There are hundreds of ways to kneel and kiss the ground.

—Translated by Coleman Barks

I Am Not I

Juan Ramón Jiménez

I am not I.
         I am this one
Walking beside me whom I do not see,
Whom at times I manage to visit,
And whom at other times I forget;
The one who remains silent when I talk,
The one who forgives, sweet, when I hate,
The one who takes a walk where I am not,
The one who will remain standing when I die.

—Translated by Robert Bly

110 POEMS OF LOVE AND REVELATION

THREE TIMES MY LIFE HAS OPENED

Jane Hirshfield

Three times my life has opened.
Once, into darkness and rain.
Once, into what the body carries at all times within it and
    starts to remember each time it enters the act of love.
Once, to the fire that holds all.
These three were not different.
You will recognize what I am saying or you will not.
But outside my window all day a maple has stepped
    from her leaves like a woman in love with winter, dropping
    the colored silks.
Neither are we different in what we know.
There is a door. It opens. Then it is closed. But a slip of
    light stays, like a scrap of unreadable paper left on the floor,
    or the one red leaf the snow releases in March.

THAT DAY

Denise Levertov

Across a lake in Switzerland, fifty years ago,
light was jousting with long lances, fencing with
    broadswords
back and forth among cloudy peaks and foothills.
We watched from a small pavilion, my mother and I,
enthralled.
             And then, behold, a shaft, a column,
a defined body, not of light but of silver rain,
formed and set out from the distant shore, leaving behind
the silent feints and thrusts, and advanced
unswervingly, at a steady pace,
toward us.
             I knew this! I'd seen it! Not the sensation
of déjà vu: it was Blake's inkwash vision,
'The Spirit of God Moving Upon the Face of the Waters'!
The column steadily came on
across the lake toward us; on each side of it,
there was no rain. We rose to our feet, breathless—
and then it reached us, took us
into its veil of silver, wrapped us
in finest weave of wet,
and we laughed for joy, astonished.

MILKWEED

James Wright

While I stood here, in the open, lost in myself,
I must have looked a long time
Down the corn rows, beyond grass,
The small house,
White walls, animals lumbering toward the barn.
I look down now. It is all changed.
Whatever it was I lost, whatever I wept for
Was a wild, gentle thing, the small dark eyes
Loving me in secret.
It is here. At a touch of my hand,
The air fills with delicate creatures
From the other world.

My Fiftieth Year

W. B. Yeats

My fiftieth year had come and gone,
I sat, a solitary man,
In a crowded London shop,
An open book and empty cup
On the marble table-top.

While on the shop and street I gazed
My body of a sudden blazed;
And twenty minutes more or less
It seemed, so great my happiness,
That I was blessèd and could bless.

So Much Happiness

Naomi Shihab Nye

for Michael

It is difficult to know what to do with so much happiness.
With sadness there is something to rub against,
a wound to tend with lotion and cloth.
When the world falls in around you, you have pieces to
    pick up,
something to hold in your hands, like ticket stubs
    or change.

But happiness floats.
It doesn't need you to hold it down.
It doesn't need anything.
Happiness lands on the roof of the next house, singing,
and disappears when it wants to.
You are happy either way.
Even the fact that you once lived in a peaceful tree house
and now live over a quarry of noise and dust
cannot make you unhappy.
Everything has a life of its own,
it too could wake up filled with possibilities
of coffee cake and ripe peaches,
and love even the floor which needs to be swept,
the soiled linens and scratched records . . .

Since there is no place large enough
to contain so much happiness,
you shrug, you raise your hands, and it flows out of you
into everything you touch. You are not responsible.
You take no credit, as the night sky takes no credit
for the moon, but continues to hold it, and share it,
and in that way, be known.

On Foot I Had to Walk Through the Solar Systems

Edith Södergran

On foot
I had to walk through the solar systems,
before I found the first thread of my red dress.
Already, I sense myself.
Somewhere in space hangs my heart,
sparks fly from it, shaking the air,
to other reckless hearts.

—Translated by Stina Katchadourian

SUNSET

Rainer Maria Rilke

Slowly the west reaches for clothes of new colors
which it passes to a row of ancient trees.
You look, and soon these two worlds both leave you,
one part climbs toward heaven, one sinks to earth,

leaving you, not really belonging to either,
not so hopelessly dark as that house that is silent,
not so unswervingly given to the eternal as that thing
that turns to a star each night and climbs—

leaving you (it is impossible to untangle the threads)
your own life, timid and standing high and growing,
so that, sometimes blocked in, sometimes reaching out,
one moment your life is a stone in you, and the next, a star.

—Translated by Robert Bly

THE WIND, ONE BRILLIANT DAY

Antonio Machado

The wind, one brilliant day, called
to my soul with an odor of jasmine.

"In return for the odor of my jasmine,
I'd like all the odor of your roses."

"I have no roses; all the flowers
in my garden are dead."

"Well then, I'll take the withered petals
and the yellow leaves and the waters of the fountain."

The wind left. And I wept. And I said to myself:
"What have you done with the garden that was entrusted to you?"

—Translated by Robert Bly

EVERYTHING IS PLUNDERED

Anna Akhmatova

Everything is plundered, betrayed, sold,
Death's great black wing scrapes the air,
Misery gnaws to the bone.
Why then do we not despair?

By day, from the surrounding woods,
cherries blow summer into town;
at night the deep transparent skies
glitter with new galaxies.

And the miraculous comes so close
to the ruined, dirty houses—
something not known to anyone at all,
but wild in our breast for centuries.

—Translated by Stanley Kunitz with Max Hayward

WEATHERING
Fleur Adcock

My face catches the wind
from the snow line
and flushes with a flush
that will never wholly settle.
Well, that was a metropolitan vanity,
wanting to look young forever, to pass.
I was never a pre-Raphaelite beauty
and only pretty enough to be seen
with a man who wanted to be seen
with a passable woman.

But now that I am in love
with a place that doesn't care
how I look and if I am happy,
happy is how I look and that's all.
My hair will grow grey in any case,
my nails chip and flake,
my waist thicken, and the years
work all their usual changes.

If my face is to be weather beaten as well,
it's little enough lost
for a year among the lakes and vales
where simply to look out my window
at the high pass
makes me indifferent to mirrors
and to what my soul may wear
over its new complexion.

Is My Soul Asleep?

Antonio Machado

Is my soul asleep?
Have those beehives that work
in the night stopped? And the water-
wheel of thought, is it
going around now, cups
empty, carrying only shadows?

No, my soul is not asleep.
It is awake, wide awake.
It neither sleeps nor dreams, but watches,
its eyes wide open
far-off things, and listens
at the shores of the great silence.

—Translated by Robert Bly

I Have Many Brothers in the South

Rainer Maria Rilke

I have many brothers in the South.
Laurels stand there in monastery gardens.
I know in what a human way they imagine the Madonna,
and I think often of young Titians
through whom God walks burning.

Yet no matter how deeply I go down into myself
my God is dark, and like a webbing made
of a hundred roots, that drink in silence.
I know that my trunk rose from his warmth, but that's all,
because my branches hardly move at all
near the ground, and just wave a little in the wind.

—Translated by Robert Bly

SWEET DARKNESS

David Whyte

When your eyes are tired
the world is tired also.

When your vision has gone
no part of the world can find you.

Time to go into the dark
where the night has eyes
to recognize its own.

There you can be sure
you are not beyond love.

The dark will be your womb
tonight.

The night will give you a horizon
further than you can see.

You must learn one thing.
The world was made to be free in.

Give up all the other worlds
except the one to which you belong.

Oceans
Juan Ramón Jiménez

I have a feeling that my boat
has struck, down there in the depths,
against a great thing.
                              And nothing
happens! Nothing . . . Silence . . . Waves. . . .

—Nothing happens? Or has everything hap-
pened,
and are we standing now, quietly, in the new life?

—Translated by Robert Bly

WATER

Philip Larkin

If I were called in
To construct a religion
I should make use of water.

Going to church
Would entail a fording
To dry, different clothes;

My liturgy would employ
Images of sousing,
A furious devout drench,

And I should raise in the east
A glass of water
Where any-angled light
Would congregate endlessly.

THE LONG BOAT

Stanley Kunitz

When his boat snapped loose
from its moorings, under
the screaking of the gulls,
he tried at first to wave
to his dear ones on shore,
but in the rolling fog
they had already lost their faces.
Too tired even to choose
between jumping and calling,
somehow he felt absolved and free
of his burdens, those mottoes
stamped on his name-tag:
conscience, ambition, and all
that caring.
He was content to lie down
with the family ghosts
in the slop of his cradle,
buffeted by the storm,
endlessly drifting.
Peace! Peace!
To be rocked by the Infinite!
As if it didn't matter
which way was home;
as if he didn't know
he loved the earth so much
he wanted to stay forever.

YOU SEE I WANT A LOT

Rainer Maria Rilke

You see, I want a lot.
Perhaps I want everything:
the darkness that comes with every infinite fall
and the shivering blaze of every step up.

So many live on and want nothing,
and are raised to the rank of prince
by the slippery ease of their light judgments.

But what you love to see are faces
that do work and feel thirst.

You love most of all those who need you
as they need a crowbar or a hoe.

You have not grown old, and it is not too late
to dive into your increasing depths
where life calmly gives out its own secret.

—Translated by Robert Bly

THE JOURNEY

Mary Oliver

One day you finally knew
what you had to do, and began,
though the voices around you
kept shouting
their bad advice—
though the whole house
began to tremble
and you felt the old tug
at your ankles.
"Mend my life!"
each voice cried.
But you didn't stop.
You knew what you had to do,
though the wind pried
with its stiff fingers
at the very foundations,
though their melancholy
was terrible.
It was already late
enough, and a wild night,
and the road full of fallen
branches and stones.
But little by little,
as you left their voices behind,
the stars began to burn
through the sheets of clouds,
and there was a new voice
which you slowly
recognized as your own,

that kept you company
as you strode deeper and deeper
into the world,
determined to do
the only thing you could do—
determined to save
the only life you could save.

I Take Master Card (Charge Your Love to Me)

Nikki Giovanni

I've heard all the stories
'bout how you don't deserve me
'cause I'm so strong and beautiful and wonderful and you
    could
never live up to what you know I should have but I just want
    to let you know:

I take Master Card

You can love me as much as your heart can stand
then put the rest on
account and pay the interest
each month until we get this settled

You see we modern women do comprehend
that we deserve a whole lot more
than what is normally being offered but we are trying
to get aligned with the modern world

So baby you can love me all
you like 'cause you're pre-approved
and you don't have to sign on
the bottom line

Charge it up
'til we just can't take no more
it's the modern way

I take Master Card
to see your Visa
and I deal with a Discovery but I don't want any American
Express 'cause like the Pointer Sisters say: I need a slow hand.

THE GREATEST LOVE

Anna Swir

She is sixty. She lives
the greatest love of her life.

She walks arm-in-arm with her dear one,
her hair streams in the wind.
Her dear one says:
"You have hair like pearls."

Her children say:
"Old fool."

—Translated by Czeslaw Milosz and Leonard Nathan

Rapture

Galway Kinnell

I can feel she has got out of bed.
That means it is seven A.M.
I have been lying with eyes shut,
thinking, or possibly dreaming,
of how she might look if, at breakfast,
I spoke about the hidden place in her
which, to me, is like a soprano's tremolo,
and right then, over toast and bramble jelly,
if such things are possible, she came.
I imagine she would show it while trying to conceal it.
I imagine her hair would fall about her face
and she would become apparently downcast,
as she does at a concert when she is moved.
The hypnopompic play passes, and I open my eyes
and there she is, next to the bed,
bending to a low drawer, picking over
various small smooth black, white,
and pink items of underwear. She bends
so low her back runs parallel to the earth,
but there is no sway in it, there is little burden, the day
    has hardly begun.
The two mounds of muscles for walking, leaping,
    lovemaking,
lift toward the east—what can I say?
Simile is useless; there is nothing like them on earth.
Her breasts fall full; the nipples
are deep pink in the glare shining up through the iron bars
of the gate under the earth where those who could not love
press, wanting to be born again.

I reach out and take her wrist
and she falls back into bed and at once starts unbuttoning
    my pajamas.
Later, when I open my eyes, there she is again,
rummaging in the same low drawer.
The clock shows eight. Hmmm.
With huge, silent effort of great,
mounded muscles the earth has been turning.
She takes a piece of silken cloth
from the drawer and stands up. Under the falls
of hair her face has become quiet and downcast,
as if she will be, all day among strangers,
looking down inside herself at our rapture.

LINES COMPOSED A FEW MILES ABOVE TINTERN ABBEY (EXCERPT)

William Wordsworth

                    And I have felt
A presence that disturbs me with the joy
Of elevated thoughts; a sense sublime
Of something far more deeply interfused,
Whose dwelling is the light of setting suns,
And the round ocean and the living air,
And the blue sky, and in the mind of man:
A motion and a spirit, that impels
All thinking things, all objects of all thought,
And rolls through all things.

RISKING EVERYTHING

A HOMECOMING

Wendell Berry

One faith is bondage. Two
are free. In the trust
of old love, cultivation shows
a dark and graceful wilderness
at its heart. Wild
in that wilderness, we roam
the distance of our faith;
safe beyond the bounds
of what we know. O love,
open. Show me
my country. Take me home.

THE VERY SHORT SUTRA ON THE MEETING OF THE BUDDHA AND THE GODDESS

Rick Fields

Thus I have made up:

Once the Buddha was walking along along the
forest path in the Oak Grove at Ojai, walking
without arriving anywhere or having any thought
of arriving or not arriving

and lotuses shining with the morning dew
miraculously appeared under every step
soft as silk beneath the toes of the Buddha

When suddenly, out of the turquoise sky,
dancing in front of his half-shut inward-looking
eyes, shimmering like a rainbow
or a spider's web
transparent as the dew on a lotus flower,

—the Goddess appeared quivering like a
hummingbird in the air before him

She, for she was surely a she
as the Buddha could clearly see
with his eye of discriminating awareness wisdom,

was mostly red in color though when the light
shifted she flashed like a rainbow.

She was naked except for the usual flower
ornaments Goddesses wear

Her long hair was deep blue, her two eyes
fathomless pits of space and her third eye a
bloodshot ring of fire.

The Buddha folded his hands together
and greeted the Goddess thus.

"O Goddess, why are you blocking my path.
Before I saw you I was happily going nowhere.
Now I'm not sure where to go."

"You can go around me," said the Goddess,
twirling on her heels like a bird darting away, but
just a little way away, "or you can come after me.
This is my forest too, you can't pretend I'm not
here."

With that the Buddha sat supple as a snake solid
as a rock beneath a Bo tree that sprang full-leaved
to shade him.

"Perhaps we should have a chat," he said.

"After years of arduous practice at the time of the
morning star I penetrated reality, and now . . ."

"Not so fast. Buddha.
I *am* reality."

The Earth stood still, the oceans paused,

the wind itself listened—a thousand arhats,
bodhisattvas, and dakinis magically appeared to
hear what would happen in the conversation.

I know I take my life in my hands," said the
Buddha. "But I am known as the Fearless One
—so here goes."

And he and the Goddess without further words
exchanged glances.

Light rays like sunbeams shot forth so bright that
even Sariputra, the All-Seeing One, had to turn
away.

And then they exchanged thoughts and the
illumination was as bright as a diamond candle.

And then they exchanged mind

And there was a great silence as vast as the universe
that contains everything

And then they exchanged bodies

And clothes

And the Buddha arose as the Goddess
and the Goddess arose as the Buddha

and so on back and forth for a hundred thousand
hundred thousand kalpas.

If you meet the Buddha you meet the Goddess. If
you meet the Goddess you meet the Buddha

Not only that. This: The Buddha is the Goddess,
the Goddess is the Buddha.

And not only that. This: The Buddha is emptiness
the Goddess is bliss, the Goddess is emptiness the
Buddha is bliss.

And that is what and what-not you are. It's true.

So here comes the mantra of the Goddess and the
Buddha, the unsurpassed non-dual mantra. Just to
say this mantra, just to hear this mantra once, just
to hear one word of this mantra once makes
everything the way it truly is: OK.

So here it is:
Earth-walker/sky-walker
   Hey, silent one, Hey, great talker
Not two/Not one
   Not separate/Not apart
This is the heart
   Bliss is emptiness
   Emptiness is bliss

Be your breath, Ah
Smile, Hey
And relax, Ho
And remember this: You can't miss.

GIFT

Czeslaw Milosz

A day so happy.
Fog lifted early, I worked in the garden.
Hummingbirds were stopping over honeysuckle flowers.
There was no thing on earth I wanted to possess.
I knew no one worth my envying him.
Whatever evil I had suffered, I forgot.
To think that once I was the same man did not
   embarrass me.
In my body I felt no pain.
When straightening up, I saw the blue sea and sails.

NOTICE

Steve Kowit

This evening, the sturdy Levis
I wore every day for over a year
& which seemed to the end in perfect condition,
suddenly tore.
How or why I don't know,
but there it was—a big rip at the crotch.
A month ago my friend Nick
walked off a racquetball court,
showered,
got into his street clothes,
& halfway home collapsed & died.
Take heed you who read this
& drop to your knees now & again
like the poet Christopher Smart
& kiss the earth & be joyful
& make much of your time
& be kindly to everyone,
even to those who do not deserve it.
For although you may not believe it will happen,
you too will one day be gone.
I, whose Levis ripped at the crotch
for no reason,
assure you that such is the case.
Pass it on.

THINGS TO THINK

Robert Bly

Think in ways you've never thought before
If the phone rings, think of it as carrying a message
Larger than anything you've ever heard,
Vaster than a hundred lines of Yeats.

Think that someone may bring a bear to your door,
Maybe wounded and deranged; or think that a moose
Has risen out of the lake, and he's carrying on his antlers
A child of your own whom you've never seen.

When someone knocks on the door, think that he's about
To give you something large: tell you you're forgiven,
Or that it's not necessary to work all the time, or that it's
Been decided that if you lie down no one will die.

It's Possible

Antonio Machado

It's possible that while sleeping the hand
that sows the seeds of stars
started the ancient music going again

—like a note from a great harp—
and the frail wave came to our lips
as one or two honest words.

—Translated by Robert Bly

THE THIRD BODY

Robert Bly

A man and a woman sit near each other, and they do
    not long
At this moment to be older, or younger, or born
In any other nation, or any other time, or any other
    place.
They are content to be where they are, talking or not
    talking.
Their breaths together feed someone whom we do
    not know.
The man sees the way his fingers move;
He sees her hands close around a book she hands to
    him.
They obey a third body that they share in common.
They have promised to love that body.
Age may come; parting may come; death will come!
A man and a woman sit near each other;
As they breathe they feed someone we do not know,
Someone we know of, whom we have never seen.

Dithyramb of a Happy Woman

Anna Swir

Song of excess,
strength, mighty tenderness,
pliant ecstasy.
Magnificence
lovingly dancing.

I quiver as a body in rapture,
I quiver as a wing,
I am an explosion,
I overstep myself,
I am a fountain,
I have its resilience.
Excess,
a thousand excesses,
strength,
song of gushing strength.

There are gifts in me,
flowerings of abundance,
curls of light are sobbing,
a flame is foaming, its lofty ripeness
is ripening.
Oceans of glare,
rosy as the palate
of a big mouth in ecstasy.

I am astonished
up to my nostrils, I snort,
a snorting universe of astonishment
inundates me.
I am gulping excess, I am choking with fullness,
I am impossible as reality.

—Translated by Czeslaw Milosz

I Unpetalled You

Juan Ramón Jiménez

I unpetalled you, like a rose,
to see your soul,
and I didn't see it.

               But everything around
—horizons of lands and of seas—,
everything, out to the infinite,
was filled with a fragrance,
enormous and alive.

—Translated by Stephen Mitchell

To have without holding

Marge Piercy

Learning to love differently is hard,
love with the hands wide open, love
with the doors banging on their hinges,
the cupboard unlocked, the wind
roaring and whimpering in the rooms
rustling the sheets and snapping the blinds
that thwack like rubber bands
in an open palm.

It hurts to love wide open
stretching the muscles that feel
as if they are made of wet plaster,
then of blunt knives, then
of sharp knives.

It hurts to thwart the reflexes
of grab, of clutch; to love and let
go again and again. It pesters to remember
the lover who is not in the bed,
to hold back what is owed to the work
that gutters like a candle in a cave
without air, to love consciously,
conscientiously, concretely, constructively.

I can't do it, you say it's killing
me, but you thrive, you glow
on the street like a neon raspberry,
you float and sail, a helium balloon
bright bachelor's button blue and bobbing

on the cold and hot winds of our breath,
as we make and unmake in passionate
diastole and systole the rhythm
of our unbound bonding, to have
and not to hold, to love
with minimized malice, hunger
and anger moment by moment balanced.

Deeper Than Love

D. H. Lawrence

There is love, and it is a deep thing
but there are deeper things than love.

First and last, man is alone.
He is born alone, and alone he dies
and alone he is while he lives, in his deepest self.

Love, like the flowers, is life, growing.
But underneath are the deep rocks, the living rock that lives
     alone
and deeper still the unknown fire, unknown and heavy, heavy
and alone.

Love is a thing of twoness.
But underneath any twoness, man is alone.

And underneath the great turbulent emotions of love, the
     violent herbage,
lies the living rock of a single creature's pride,
the dark, naïf pride.
And deeper even than the bedrock of pride
lies the ponderous fire of naked life
with its strange primordial consciousness of justice
and its primordial consciousness of connection,
connection with still deeper, still more terrible life-fire
and the old, old final life-truth.

Love is of twoness, and is lovely
like the living life on the earth

but below all roots of love lies the bedrock of naked pride,
    subterranean,
and deeper than the bedrock of pride is the primordial fire of
    the middle
which rests in connection with the further forever unknowable
    fire of all things
and which rocks with a sense of connection, religion
and trembles with a sense of truth, primordial consciousness
and is silent with a sense of justice, the fiery primordial
    imperative.

All this is deeper than love
deeper than love.

ALL I WAS DOING WAS BREATHING

Mirabai

Something has reached out and taken in the beams of my eyes.
There is a longing, it is for his body, for every hair of that
    dark body.
All I was doing was being, and the Dancing Energy came by
    my house.
His face looks curiously like the moon, I saw it from the side,
    smiling.
My family says: "Don't ever see him again!" And implies things
    in a low voice.
But my eyes have their own life; they laugh at rules, and know
    whose they are.
I believe I can bear on my shoulders whatever you want to
    say of me.
Mira says: Without the energy that lifts mountains, how am I
    to live?

—Translated by Robert Bly

SOUL AT THE WHITE HEAT

Emily Dickinson

Dare you see a Soul *at the White Heat*?
Then crouch within the door—
Red—is the Fire's common tint—
But when the vivid Ore
Has vanquished Flame's conditions,
It quivers from the Forge
Without a color, but the light
Of unanointed Blaze.
Least Village has its Blacksmith
Whose Anvil's even ring
Stands symbol for the finer Forge
That soundless tugs—within—
Refining these impatient Ores
With Hammer, and with Blaze
Until the Designated Light
Repudiate the Forge—

WILD NIGHTS

Emily Dickinson

Wild Nights—Wild Nights!
Were I with thee
Wild Nights should be
Our luxury!

Futile—the Winds—
To a Heart in port—
Done with the Compass—
Done with the Chart!

Rowing in Eden—
Ah, the Sea!
Might I but moor—Tonight—
In Thee!

I THANK YOU

E. E. Cummings

i thank You God for most this amazing
day:for the leaping greenly spirits of trees
and a blue true dream of sky;and for everything
which is natural which is infinite which is yes

(i who have died am alive again today,
and this is the sun's birthday;this is the birth
day of life and of love and wings:and of the gay
great happening illimitably earth)

how should tasting touching hearing seeing
breathing any—lifted from the no
of all nothing—human merely being
doubt unimaginable You?

(now the ears of my ears awake and
now the eyes of my eyes are opened)

A BLESSING
James Wright

Just off the highway to Rochester, Minnesota,
Twilight bounds softly forth on the grass.
And the eyes of those two Indian ponies
Darken with kindness.
They have come gladly out of the willows
To welcome my friend and me.
We step over the barbed wire into the pasture
Where they have been grazing all day, alone.
They ripple tensely, they can hardly contain their
    happiness
That we have come.
They bow shyly as wet swans. They love each other.
There is no loneliness like theirs.
At home once more,
They begin munching the young tufts of spring in the darkness.
I would like to hold the slenderer one in my arms,
For she has walked over to me
And nuzzled my left hand.
She is black and white,
Her mane falls wild on her forehead,
And the light breeze moves me to caress her long ear
That is delicate as the skin over a girl's wrist.
Suddenly I realize
That if I stepped out of my body I would break
Into blossom.

POSTSCRIPT

Seamus Heaney

And some time make the time to drive out west
Into County Clare, along the Flaggy Shore,
In September or October, when the wind
And the light are working off each other
So that the ocean on one side is wild
With foam and glitter, and inland among stones
The surface of a slate-grey lake is lit
By the earthed lightning of a flock of swans,
Their feathers roughed and ruffling, white on white,
Their fully grown headstrong-looking heads
Tucked or cresting or busy underwater.
Useless to think you'll park and capture it
More thoroughly. You are neither here nor there,
A hurry through which known and strange things pass
As big soft buffetings come at the car sideways
And catch the heart off guard and blow it open.

RIPENESS

Jane Hirshfield

Ripeness is
what falls away with ease.
Not only the heavy apple,
the pear,
but also the dried brown strands
of autumn iris from their core.

To let your body
love this world
that gave itself to your care
in all of its ripeness,
with ease,
and will take itself from you
in equal ripeness and ease,
is also harvest.

And however sharply
you are tested—
this sorrow, that great love—
it too will leave on that clean knife.

IN BLACKWATER WOODS

Mary Oliver

Look, the trees
are turning
their own bodies
into pillars

of light,
are giving off the rich
fragrance of cinnamon
and fulfillment,

the long tapers
of cattails
are bursting and floating away over
the blue shoulders

of the ponds,
and every pond,
no matter what its
name is, is

nameless now.
Every year
everything
I have ever learned

in my lifetime
leads back to this: the fires
and the black river of loss
whose other side

is salvation,
whose meaning
none of us will ever know.
To live in this world

you must be able
to do three things:
to love what is mortal;
to hold it

against your bones knowing
your own life depends on it;
and, when the time comes to let it go,
to let it go.

PARKINSON'S DISEASE

Galway Kinnell

While spoon-feeding him with one hand
she holds his hand with her other hand,
or rather lets it rest on top of his,
which is permanently clenched shut.
When he turns his head away, she reaches
around and puts in the spoonful blind.
He will not accept the next morsel
until he has completely chewed this one.
His bright squint tells her he finds
the shrimp she has just put in delicious.
She strokes his head very slowly, as if
to cheer up each hair sticking up
from its root in his stricken brain.
Standing behind him, she presses
her cheek to his, kisses his jowl,
and his eyes seem to stop seeing
and do nothing but emit light.
Could heaven be a time, after we are dead,
of remembering the knowledge
flesh had from flesh? The flesh
of his face is hard, perhaps
from years spent facing down others
until they fell back, and harder
from years of being himself faced down
and falling back, and harder still
from all the while frowning
and beaming and worrying and shouting
and probably letting go in rages.
His face softens into a kind

of quizzical wince, as if one
of the other animals were working at
getting the knack of the human smile.
When picking up a cookie he uses
both thumbtips to grip it
and push it against an index finger
to secure it so that he can lift it.
She takes him to the bathroom,
and when they come out, she is facing him,
walking backwards in front of him
holding his hands, pulling him
when he stops, reminding him to step
when he forgets and starts to pitch forward.
She is leading her old father into the future
as far as they can go, and she is walking
him back into her childhood, where she stood
in bare feet on the toes of his shoes
and they foxtrotted on this same rug.
I watch them closely: she could be teaching him
the last steps that one day she may teach me.
At this moment, he glints and shines,
as if it will be only a small dislocation
for him to pass from this paradise into the next.

KINDNESS
Naomi Shihab Nye

Before you know what kindness really is
you must lose things,
feel the future dissolve in a moment
like salt in a weakened broth.
What you held in your hand,
what you counted and carefully saved,
all this must go so you know
how desolate the landscape can be
between the regions of kindness.
How you ride and ride
thinking the bus will never stop,
the passengers eating maize and chicken
will stare out the window forever.

Before you learn the tender gravity of kindness,
you must travel where the Indian in a white poncho
lies dead by the side of the road.
You must see how this could be you,
how he too was someone
who journeyed through the night with plans
and the simple breath that kept him alive.

Before you know kindness as the deepest thing inside,
You must know sorrow as the other deepest thing.
You must wake up with sorrow.
You must speak to it till your voice
catches the thread of all sorrows
and you see the size of the cloth.

Then it is only kindness that makes sense anymore,
only kindness that ties your shoes
and sends you out into the day to mail letters and purchase bread,
only kindness that raises its head
from the crowd of the world to say
It is I you have been looking for,
and then goes with you everywhere
like a shadow or a friend.

Colombia

FOR THE SAKE OF STRANGERS

Dorianne Laux

No matter what the grief, its weight,
we are obliged to carry it.
We rise and gather momentum, the dull strength
that pushes us through crowds.
And then the young boy gives me directions
so avidly. A woman holds the glass door open,
waits patiently for my empty body to pass through.
All day it continues, each kindness
reaching toward another—a stranger
singing to no one as I pass on the path, trees
offering their blossoms, a retarded child
who lifts his almond eyes and smiles.
Somehow they always find me, seem even
to be waiting, determined to keep me
from myself, from the thing that calls to me
as it must have once called to them—
this temptation to step off the edge
and fall weightless, away from the world.

The Same Inside

Anna Swir

Walking to your place for a love feast
I saw at a street corner
an old beggar woman.

I took her hand,
kissed her delicate cheek,
we talked, she was
the same inside as I am,
from the same kind,
I sensed this instantly
as a dog knows by scent
another dog.

I gave her money.
I could not part from her.
After all, one needs
someone who is close.

And then I no longer knew
why I was walking to your place.

—Translated by Czeslaw Milosz and Leonard Nathan

ODDJOB, A BULL TERRIER

Derek Walcott

You prepare for one sorrow,
but another comes.
It is not like the weather,
you cannot brace yourself,
the unreadiness is all.
Your companion, the woman,
the friend next to you,
the child at your side,
and the dog,
we tremble for them,
we look seaward and muse
it will rain.
We shall get ready for rain;
you do not connect
the sunlight altering
the darkening oleanders
in the sea-garden,
the gold going out of the palms.
You do not connect this,
the fleck of the drizzle
on your flesh,
with the dog's whimper,
the thunder doesn't frighten,
the readiness is all;
what follows at your feet
is trying to tell you
the silence is all:
it is deeper than the readiness,
it is sea-deep,

earth-deep,
love-deep.

The silence
is stronger than thunder,
we are stricken dumb and deep
as the animals who never utter love
as we do, except
it becomes unutterable
and must be said,
in a whimper,
in tears,
in the drizzle that comes to our eyes
not uttering the loved thing's name,
the silence of the dead,
the silence of the deepest buried love is
the one silence,
and whether we bear it for beast,
for child, for woman, or friend,
it is the one love, it is the same,
and it is blest
deepest by loss
it is blest, it is blest.

FOR THE RAINDROP
Ghalib

For the raindrop, joy is in entering the river—
Unbearable pain becomes its own cure.

Travel far enough into sorrow, tears turn to sighing;
In this way we learn how water can die into air.

When, after heavy rain, the stormclouds disperse,
Is it not that they've wept themselves clear to the end?

If you want to know the miracle, how wind can polish
    a mirror,
Look: the shining glass grows green in spring.

It's the rose's unfolding, Ghalib, that creates the desire to see—
In every color and circumstance, may the eyes be open for what comes.

—Translated by Jane Hirshfield

A Place to Sit

Kabir

Don't go outside your house to see flowers.
My friend, don't bother with that excursion.
Inside your body there are flowers.
One flower has a thousand petals.
That will do for a place to sit.
Sitting there you will have a glimpse of beauty
inside the body and out of it,
before gardens and after gardens.

—Translated by Robert Bly

110 POEMS OF LOVE AND REVELATION

BREATH
Kabir

Are you looking for me? I am in the next seat.
My shoulder is against yours.
You will not find me in stupas, not in Indian shrine rooms,
  nor in synagogues, nor in cathedrals:
not in masses, nor kirtans, not in legs winding around your
  own neck, nor in eating nothing but vegetables.
When you really look for me, you will see me instantly—
you will find me in the tiniest house of time.
Kabir says: Student, tell me, what is God?
He is the breath inside the breath.

—Translated by Robert Bly

WHEN THE SHOE FITS

Chuang Tzu

Ch'ui the draftsman
Could draw more perfect circles freehand
Than with a compass.

His fingers brought forth
Spontaneous forms from nowhere. His mind
Was meanwhile free and without concern
With what he was doing.

No application was needed
His mind was perfectly simple
And knew no obstacle.

So, when the shoe fits
The foot is forgotten,
When the belt fits
The belly is forgotten,
When the heart is right
"For" and "against" are forgotten.

No drives, no compulsions,
No needs, no attractions:
Then your affairs
Are under control.
You are a free man.

Easy is right. Begin right
And you are easy.
Continue easy and you are right.

The right way to go easy
Is to forget the right way
And forget that the going is easy.

—Translated by Thomas Merton

Sometimes a Man

Rainer Maria Rilke

Sometimes a man stands up during supper
and walks outdoors, and keeps on walking,
because of a church that stands somewhere in the East.

And his children say blessings on him as if he were dead.

And another man, who remains inside his own house,
dies there, inside the dishes and in the glasses,
so that his children have to go far out into the world
toward that same church, which he forgot.

—Translated by Robert Bly

THE ROAD NOT TAKEN

Robert Frost

Two roads diverged in a yellow wood,
And sorry I could not travel both
And be one traveler, long I stood
And looked down one as far as I could
To where it bent in the undergrowth;

Then took the other, as just as fair,
And having perhaps the better claim,
Because it was grassy and wanted wear;
Though as for that the passing there
Had worn them really about the same,

And both that morning equally lay
In leaves no step had trodden black.
Oh, I kept the first for another day!
Yet knowing how way leads on to way,
I doubted if I should ever come back.

I shall be telling this with a sigh
Somewhere ages and ages hence:
Two roads diverged in a wood, and I—
I took the one less traveled by,
And that has made all the difference.

The Well of Grief

David Whyte

Those who will not slip beneath
   the still surface on the well of grief

turning downward through its black water
   to the place we cannot breathe

will never know the source from which we drink,
   the secret water, cold and clear,

nor find in the darkness glimmering
   the small round coins
      thrown by those who wished for something else.

—From *Where Many Rivers Meet*

ENCOUNTER

Czeslaw Milosz

We were riding through frozen fields in a wagon at dawn.
A red wing rose in the darkness.

And suddenly a hare ran across the road.
One of us pointed to it with his hand.

That was long ago. Today neither of them is alive,
Not the hare, nor the man who made the gesture.

O my love, where are they, where are they going
The flash of a hand, streak of movement, rustle of pebbles.
I ask not out of sorrow, but in wonder.

THE PROMISE

Marie Howe

In the dream I had when he came back not sick
but whole, and wearing his winter coat,

he looked at me as though he couldn't speak, as if
there were a law against it, a membrane he couldn't break.

His silence was what he could not
not do, like our breathing in this world, like our living,

as we do, in time.
And I told him: I'm reading all this Buddhist stuff,

and listen, we don't die when we die. Death is an event,
a threshold we pass through. We go on and on

and into light forever.
And he looked down, and then back up at me. It was the
   look we'd pass

across the kitchen table when Dad was drunk again and
   dangerous,
the level look that wants to tell you something,

in a crowded room, something important, and can't.

O Taste and See

Denise Levertov

The world is
not with us enough.
O taste and see

the subway Bible poster said,
meaning **The Lord**, meaning
if anything all that lives
to the imagination's tongue,

grief, mercy, language,
tangerine, weather, to
breathe them, bite,
savor, chew, swallow, transform

into our flesh our
deaths, crossing the street, plum, quince,
living in the orchard and being

hungry, and plucking
the fruit.

OATMEAL
Galway Kinnell

I eat oatmeal for breakfast.
I make it on the hot plate and put skimmed milk on it.
I eat it alone.
I am aware it is not good to eat oatmeal alone.
Its consistency is such that it is better for your mental health
    if somebody eats it with you.
That is why I often think up an imaginary companion to have
    breakfast with.
Possibly it is even worse to eat oatmeal with an imaginary
    companion.
Nevertheless, yesterday morning, I ate my oatmeal with
    John Keats.
Keats said I was right to invite him: due to its glutinous
    texture, gluey lumpishness, hint of slime, and unusual
    willingness to disintegrate, oatmeal must never be
    eaten alone.
He said it is perfectly OK, however, to eat it with an
    imaginary companion,
and he himself had enjoyed memorable porridges with
    Edmund Spenser and John Milton.
He also told me about writing the "Ode to a Nightingale."
He wrote it quickly, he said, on scraps of paper, which he
    then stuck in his pocket,
but when he got home he couldn't figure out the order of the
    stanzas, and he and a friend spread the papers on a table,
    and they made some sense of them, but he isn't sure to this
    day if they got it right.
He still wonders about the occasional sense of drift between
    stanzas,

and the way here and there a line will go into the configuration
of a Moslem at prayer, then raise itself up and peer about,
then lay itself down slightly off the mark, causing the poem
to move forward with God's reckless wobble.
He said someone told him that in life Wordsworth heard
about the scraps of paper on the table, and tried shuffling
some stanzas of his own, but only made matters worse.
When breakfast was over, John recited "To Autumn."
He recited it slowly, with much feeling, and he articulated the
words lovingly, and his odd accent sounded sweet.
He didn't offer the story of writing "To Autumn," I doubt if
there is much of one.
But he did say the sight of a just-harvested oat field got him
started on it and two of the lines, "For Summer has o'er-
brimmed their clammy cells" and "Thou watchest the last
oozings hours by hours," came to him while eating oatmeal
alone.
I can see him—drawing a spoon through the stuff, gazing into
the glimmering furrows, muttering—and it occurs to me:
maybe there is no sublime, only the shining of the amnion's
tatters.
For supper tonight I am going to have a baked potato left
over from lunch.
I'm aware that a leftover baked potato can be damp, slippery,
and simultaneously gummy and crumbly,
and therefore I'm going to invite Patrick Kavanagh to join me.

ODE TO MY SUIT

Pablo Neruda

Every morning you wait
on a chair, suit,
for my vanity, my love,
my hope, my body
to fill you.
I have hardly
emerged from sleep,
I leave the water,
I enter your sleeves,
my legs search for
the hollow of your legs,
and thus embraced
by your untiring loyalty
I go out to walk the pasture,
I enter poetry,
I look through the windows,
things,
men, women,
events and struggles
keep shaping me,
keep confronting me,
making my hands work,
opening my eyes,
wearing out my mouth,
and thus,
suit,
I also keep shaping you,
pushing out your elbows,
tearing your threads,

and thus your life grows
in the image of my life.
You flap and rustle
in the wind
as if you were my soul,
at bad moments
you cling
to my bones,
empty, at night
darkness and dream
people with their phantoms
your wings and mine.
I ask
whether someday
a bullet
from the enemy
will stain you with my blood
and then
you will die with me
or perhaps
it may not be
so dramatic
but simple,
and you will gradually get sick,
suit,
with me,
you will grow old
with me, with my body,
and together
we will enter
the earth.

That's why
every day
I greet you
with reverence and then
you embrace me and I forget you,
because we are one
and we will go on facing
the wind, at night,
the streets or the struggle,
one body,
perhaps, perhaps, motionless someday.

—Translated by Stephen Mitchell

SNAKE

D. H. Lawrence

A snake came to my water-trough
On a hot, hot day, and I in pyjamas for the heat,
To drink there.

In the deep, strange-scented shade of the great dark
  carob-tree
I came down the steps with my pitcher
And must wait, must stand and wait, for there he was at
  the trough before me.

He reached down from a fissure in the earth-wall in the
  gloom
And trailed his yellow-brown slackness soft-bellied down,
  over the edge of the stone trough
And rested his throat upon the stone bottom,
And where the water had dripped from the tap, in a small
  clearness,
He sipped with his straight mouth,
Softly drank through his straight gums, into his slack long
  body,
Silently.

Someone was before me at my water-trough,
And I, like a second comer, waiting.

He lifted his head from his drinking, as cattle do,
And looked at me vaguely, as drinking cattle do,
And flickered his two-forked tongue from his lips, and
  mused a moment,

And stooped and drank a little more,
Being earth-brown, earth-golden from the burning bowels
    of the earth
On the day of Sicilian July, with Etna smoking.
The voice of my education said to me
He must be killed,
For in Sicily the black, black snakes are innocent, the gold
    are venomous.

And voices in me said, If you were a man
You would take a stick and break him now, and finish him off.

But must I confess how I liked him,
How glad I was he had come like a guest in quiet, to drink
    at my water-trough
And depart peaceful, pacified, and thankless,
Into the burning bowels of this earth?

Was it cowardice, that I dared not kill him?
Was it perversity, that I longed to talk to him?
Was it humility, to feel so honoured?
I felt so honoured.

And yet those voices:
If you were not afraid, you would kill him!

And truly I was afraid, I was most afraid,
But even so, honoured still more
That he should seek my hospitality.
From out the dark door of the secret earth.
He drank enough

And lifted his head, dreamily, as one who has drunken,
And flickered his tongue like a forked night on the air, so black,
Seeming to lick his lips,
And looked around like a god, unseeing, into the air,
And slowly turned his head,
And slowly, very slowly, as if thrice adream,
Proceeded to draw his slow length curving round
And climb again the broken bank of my wall-face.

And as he put his head into that dreadful hole,
And as he slowly drew up, snake-easing his shoulders, and
    entered farther,
A sort of horror, a sort of protest against his withdrawing
    into that horrid black hole,
Deliberately going into the blackness, and slowly drawing'
    himself after,
Overcame me now his back was turned.

I looked round, I put down my pitcher,
I picked up a clumsy log
And threw it at the water-trough with a clatter.

I think it did not hit him,
But suddenly that part of him that was left behind convulsed
    in undignified haste,
Writhed like lightning, and was gone
Into the black hole, the earth-lipped fissure in the wall-front.
At which, in the intense still noon, I stared with fascination.

And immediately I regretted it.
I thought how paltry, how vulgar, what a mean act!
I despised myself and the voices of my accursed human
  education.

And I thought of the albatross,
And I wished he would come back, my snake.

For he seemed to me again like a king,
Like a king in exile, uncrowned in the underworld,
Now due to be crowned again.

And so, I missed my chance with one of the lords
Of life.
And I have something to expiate;
A pettiness.

THE PEACE OF WILD THINGS

Wendell Berry

When despair for the world grows in me
and I wake in the night at the least sound
in fear of what my life and my children's lives may be,
I go and lie down where the wood drake
rests in his beauty on the water, and the great heron feeds.
I come into the peace of wild things
who do not tax their lives with forethought
of grief. I come into the presence of still water.
And I feel above me the day-blind stars
waiting with their light. For a time
I rest in the grace of the world, and am free.

ASK ME

William Stafford

Some time when the river is ice ask me
mistakes I have made. Ask me whether
what I have done is my life. Others
have come in their slow way into
my thought, and some have tried to help
or to hurt—ask me what difference
their strongest love or hate has made.

I will listen to what you say.
You and I can turn and look
at the silent river and wait. We know
the current is there, hidden; and there
are comings and goings from miles away
that hold the stillness exactly before us.
What the river says, that is what I say.

THE PRELUDE 1 (EXCERPT)

William Wordsworth

Dust as we are, the immortal spirit grows
Like harmony in music; there is a dark
Inscrutable workmanship that reconciles
Discordant elements, makes them cling together
In one society. How strange that all
The terrors, pains, and early miseries,
Regrets, vexations, lassitudes interfused
Within my mind, should e'er have borne a part,
And that a needful part, in making up
The calm existence that is mine when I
Am worthy of myself! Praise to the end!
Thanks to the means which Nature deigned to employ;
Whether her fearless visitings, or those
That came with soft alarm, like hurtless light
Opening the peaceful clouds; or she may use
Severer interventions, ministry
More palpable, as best might suit her aim.

One summer evening (led by her) I found
A little boat tied to a willow tree
Within a rocky cave, its usual home.
Straight I unloosed her chain, and stepping in
Pushed from the shore. It was an act of stealth
And troubled pleasure, nor without the voice
Of mountain echoes did my boat move on;
Leaving behind her still, on either side,
Small circles glittering idly in the moon,
Until they melted all into one track
Of sparkling light. But now, like one who rows,

Proud of his skill, to reach a chosen point
With an unswerving line, I fixed my view
Upon the summit of a craggy ridge,
The horizon's utmost boundary; for above
Was nothing but the stars and the gray sky.
She was an elfin pinnace; lustily
I dipped my oars into the silent lake,
And, as I rose upon the stroke, my boat
Went heaving through the water like a swan;
When, from behind that craggy steep till then
The horizon's bound, a huge peak, black and huge,
As if with voluntary power instinct,
Upreared its head. I struck and struck again,
And growing still in stature the grim shape
Towered up between me and the stars, and still,
For so it seemed, with purpose of its own
And measured motion like a living thing,
Strode after me. With trembling oars I turned,
And through the silent water stole my way
Back to the covert of the willow tree;
There in her mooring place I left my bark,
And through the meadows homeward went, in grave
And serious mood; but after I had seen
That spectacle, for many days, my brain
Worked with a dim and undetermined sense
Of unknown modes of being; o'er my thoughts
There hung a darkness, call it solitude
Or blank desertion. No familiar shapes
Remained, no pleasant images of trees,
Of sea or sky, no colors of green fields;
But huge and mighty forms, that do not live
Like living men, moved slowly through the mind
By day, and were a trouble to my dreams.

THE CELLIST

Galway Kinnell

At intermission I find her backstage
still practicing the piece coming up next.
She calls it the "solo in high dreary."
Her bow niggles at the string like a hand
stroking skin it never wanted to touch.
Probably under her scorn she is sick
that she can't do better by it. As I am,
at the dreary in me, such as the disparity
between all the tenderness I've received
and the amount I've given, and the way
I used to shrug off the imbalance
simply as how things are, as if the male
were constituted like those coffeemakers
that produce less black bitter than the quantity
of sweet clear you poured in—forgetting about
how much I spilled through unsteady walking,
and that lot I threw on the ground
in suspicion, and for fear I wasn't worthy,
and all I poured out for reasons I don't understand yet.
"Break a leg!" somebody tells her.
Back in my seat, I can see she is nervous
when she comes out; her hand shakes as she
re-dog-ears the top corners of the big pages
that look about to flop over on their own.
Now she raises the bow—its flat bundle of hair
harvested from the rear ends of horses—like a whetted
scimitar she is about to draw across a throat,
and attacks. In a back alley a cat opens
her pink-ceilinged mouth, gets netted

in full yowl, clubbed, bagged, bicycled off, haggled open,
gutted, the gut squeezed down to its highest pitch,
washed, sliced into cello strings, which bring
an ancient screaming into this duet of hair and gut.
Now she is flying—tossing back the goblets
of Saint-Amour standing empty,
half-empty, or full on the tablecloth—
like sheet music. Her knees tighten
and loosen around the big-hipped creature
wailing and groaning between them
as if in elemental amplexus.
The music seems to rise from the crater left
when heaven was torn up and taken off the earth;
more likely it comes up through her priest's dress,
up from that clump of hair which by now
may be so wet with its water, like the waters
the fishes multiplied in at Galilee, that
each wick draws a portion all the way out
to its tip and fattens a droplet on the bush
of half notes now glittering in that dark.
At last she lifts off the bow and sits back.
Her face shines with the unselfconsciousness of a cat
screaming at night and the teary radiance of one
who gives everything no matter what has been given.

THIS ONLY

Czeslaw Milosz

A valley and above it forests in autumn colors.
A voyager arrives, a map led him here.
Or perhaps memory. Once, long ago, in the sun,
When the first snow fell, riding this way
He felt joy, strong, without reason,
Joy of the eyes. Everything was the rhythm
Of shifting trees, of a bird in flight,
Of a train on the viaduct, a feast of motion.
He returns years later, has no demands.
He wants only one, most precious thing:
To see, purely and simply, without name,
Without expectations, fears, or hopes,
At the edge where there is no I or not-I.

Once Only

Denise Levertov

All which, because it was
flame and song and granted us
joy, we thought we'd do, be, revisit,
turns out to have been what it was
that *once*, only; every initiation
did not begin
a series, a build-up: the marvelous
       did happen in our lives, our stories
       are not drab with its absence: but don't
expect now to return for more. Whatever more
there will be will be
unique as those were unique. Try
to acknowledge the next
song in its body-halo of flames as utterly
present, as now or never.

THIS MUCH I DO REMEMBER

Billy Collins

It was after dinner,
You were talking to me across the table
about something or other,
a greyhound you had seen that day
or a song you liked,

and I was looking past you
over your bare shoulder
at the three oranges lying
on the kitchen counter
next to the small electric bean grinder,
which was also orange,
and the orange and white cruets for vinegar and oil.

All of which converged
into a random still life,
so fastened together by the hasp of color,
and so fixed behind the animated
foreground of your
talking and smiling,
gesturing and pouring wine,
and the camber of your shoulders

that I could feel it being painted within me,
brushed on the wall of my skull,
while the tone of your voice
lifted and fell in its flight,
and the three oranges
remained fixed on the counter

the way stars are said
to be fixed in the universe.

Then all the moments of the past
began to line up behind that moment
and all the moments to come
assembled in front of it in a long row,
giving me reason to believe
that this was a moment I had rescued
from the millions that rush out of sight
into a darkness behind the eyes.

Even after I have forgotten what year it is,
my middle name,
and the meaning of money,
I will still carry in my pocket
the small coin of that moment,
minted in the kingdom
that we pace through every day.

LIFE

Juan Ramón Jiménez

What I used to regard as a glory shut in my face,
was a door, opening
toward this clarity:
　　　　　Country without a name:

Nothing can destroy it, this road
of doors, opening, one after another,
always toward reality:
　　　　　Life without calculation!

—Translated by James Wright; from *Eternidades*

TASTING HEAVEN
Robert Bly

Some people say that every poem should have
God in it somewhere. But of course Wallace Stevens
Wasn't one of those. We live, he said, "in a world
Without heaven to follow." Shall we agree

That we taste heaven only once, when we see
Her at fifteen walking among falling leaves?
It's possible. And yet as Stevens lay dying
He invited the priest in. There, I've said it.

The priest is not an argument, only an instance.
But our gusty emotions say to me that we have
Tasted heaven many times: these delicacies
Are left over from some larger party.

THE SWAN

Rainer Maria Rilke

This clumsy living that moves lumbering
as if in ropes through what is not done
reminds us of the awkward way the swan walks.

And to die, which is a letting go
of the ground we stand on and cling to every day,
is like the swan when he nervously lets himself down

into the water, which receives him gaily
and which flows joyfully under
and after him, wave after wave,
while the swan, unmoving and marvelously calm,
is pleased to be carried, each minute more fully grown,
more like a king, composed, farther and farther on.

—Translated by Robert Bly

THE MAN WATCHING

Rainer Maria Rilke

I can tell by the way the trees beat, after
so many dull days, on my worried windowpanes
that a storm is coming,
and I hear the far-off fields say things
I can't bear without a friend,
I can't love without a sister.

The storm, the shifter of shapes, drives on
across the woods and across time,
and the world looks as if it had no age:
the landscape, like a line in the psalm book,
is seriousness and weight and eternity.

What we choose to fight is so tiny!
What fights with us is so great!
If only we would let ourselves be dominated
as things do by some immense storm,
we would become strong too, and not need names.

When we win it's with small things,
and the triumph itself makes us small.
What is extraordinary and eternal
does not *want* to be bent by us.
I mean the Angel who appeared
to the wrestlers of the Old Testament:
when the wrestlers' sinews
grew long like metal strings,
he felt them under his fingers
like chords of deep music.

Whoever was beaten by this Angel
(who often simply declined the fight)
went away proud and strengthened
and great from that harsh hand,
that kneaded him as if to change his shape.
Winning does not tempt that man.
This is how he grows: by being defeated, decisively,
by constantly greater beings.

—Translated by Robert Bly

THE RESEMBLANCE BETWEEN YOUR LIFE AND A DOG

Robert Bly

I never intended to have this life, believe me—
It just happened. You know how dogs turn up
At a farm, and they wag but can't explain.

It's good if you can accept your life—you'll notice
Your face has become deranged trying to adjust
To it. Your face thought your life would look

Like your bedroom mirror when you were ten.
That was a clear river touched by mountain wind.
Even your parents can't believe how much you've changed.

Sparrows in winter, if you've ever held one, all feathers,
Burst out of your hand with a fiery glee.
You see them later in hedges. Teachers praise you,

But you can't quite get back to the winter sparrow.
Your life is a dog. He's been hungry for miles,
Doesn't particularly like you, but gives up, and comes in.

LAST NIGHT, AS I WAS SLEEPING

Antonio Machado

Last night, as I was sleeping,
I dreamt—marvellous error!—
that a spring was breaking
out in my heart
I said: Along which secret aqueduct,
Oh water, are you coming to me,
water of a new life
that I have never drunk?

Last night, as I was sleeping,
I dreamt—marvellous error!—
that I had a beehive
here inside my heart.
And the golden bees
were making white combs
and sweet honey
from my old failures.

Last night, as I was sleeping,
I dreamt—marvellous error!—
that a fiery sun was giving
light inside my heart.
It was fiery because I felt
warmth as from a hearth,
and sun because it gave light
and brought tears to my eyes.

RISKING EVERYTHING

Last night, as I slept,
I dreamt—marvellous error!—
that it was God I had
here inside my heart.

—Translated by Robert Bly

110 POEMS OF LOVE AND REVELATION

THE UNKNOWN FLUTE

Kabir

I know the sound of the ecstatic flute,
    but I don't know whose flute it is.

A lamp burns and has neither wick nor oil.

A lily pad blossoms and is not attached to the bottom!

When one flower opens, ordinarily dozens open.

The moon bird's head is filled with nothing but thoughts of
    the moon,
and when the next rain will come is all that the rain bird
    thinks of.

Who is it we spend our entire life loving?

                     —Translated by Robert Bly

THE SOUND
Kabir

The flute of interior time is played whether we hear it or not,
What we mean by "love" is its sound coming in.
When love hits the farthest edge of excess, it reaches a
  wisdom.
And the fragrance of that knowledge!
It penetrates our thick bodies,
it goes through walls—
Its network of notes has a structure as if a million suns were
  arranged inside.
This tune has truth in it.
Where else have you heard a sound like this?

—Translated by Robert Bly

WHEN THE ONE I LOVE

Hafez

When the one I love accepts the wine,
Then the time of the false idols is over.

Whoever looks into his luminous eyes
Cries: "Someone will soon be drunk; get the police!"

I have fallen like a fish into deep water
So that the One I love will throw his net.

I have dropped in a heap on the earth,
Perhaps I will feel a touch on my hand.

How blessed is the man who like Hafez
Has tasted in his heart the wine made before Adam.

—Translated by Robert Bly

O My Friends

Mirabai

O my friends,
What can you tell me of Love,
Whose pathways are filled with strangeness?
When you offer the Great One your love,
At the first step your body is crushed.
Next be ready to offer your head as his seat.
Be ready to orbit his lamp like a moth giving in to the light,
To live in the deer as she runs toward the hunter's call,
In the partridge that swallows hot coals for love of the moon,
In the fish that, kept from the sea, happily dies.
Like a bee trapped for life in the closing of the sweet flower,
Mira has offered herself to her Lord.
She says, the single Lotus will swallow you whole.

—Translated by Jane Hirshfield

110 POEMS OF LOVE AND REVELATION

THANK YOU, MY FATE

Anna Swir

Great humility fills me,
great purity fills me,
I make love with my dear
as if I made love dying
as if I made love praying,
tears pour
over my arms and his arms.
I don't know whether this is joy
or sadness, I don't understand
what I feel, I'm crying,
I'm crying, it's humility
as if I were dead,
gratitude, I thank you, my fate,
I'm unworthy, how beautiful
my life.

—Translated by Czeslaw Milosz and Leonard Nathan

SOME KISS WE WANT

Rumi

There is some kiss we want with
our whole lives, the touch of

spirit on the body. Seawater
begs the pearl to break its shell.

And the lily, how passionately
it needs some wild darling! At

night, I open the window and ask
the moon to come and press its

face against mine. *Breathe into
me.* Close the language-door and

open the love-window. The moon
won't use the door, only the window.

—Translated by Coleman Barks

EYES

Czeslaw Milosz

My most honorable eyes. You are not in the best shape.
I receive from you an image less than sharp,
And if a color, then it's dimmed.
And you were a pack of royal hounds
With whom I would set forth in the early morning.
My wondrously quick eyes, you saw many things,
Countries and cities. Islands and oceans.
Together we greeted immense sunrises,
When the fresh air invited us to run
Along trails just dry from cold night dew.
Now what you have seen is hidden inside
And changed into memory or dreams.
Slowly I move away from the fair of this world
And I notice in myself a distaste
For monkeyish dress, shrieks, and drumbeats.
What a relief. Alone with my meditation
On the basic similarity of humans
And their tiny grain of dissimilarity.
Without eyes, my gaze is fixed on one bright point
That grows large and takes me in.

—Translated by Czeslaw Milosz, Carol Milosz, and Renata Gorczynski

LAKE AND MAPLE

Jane Hirshfield

I want to give myself
utterly
as this maple
that burned and burned
for three days without stinting
and then in two more
dropped off every leaf;
as this lake that,
no matter what comes
to its green-blue depths,
both takes and returns it.
In the still heart,
that refuses nothing,
the world is twice-born—
two earths wheeling,
two heavens,
two egrets reaching
down into subtraction;
even the fish
for an instant doubled,
before it is gone.
I want the fish.
I want the losing it all
when it rains and I want
the returning transparence.
I want the place
by the edge-flowers where
the shallow sand is deceptive,
where whatever

steps in must plunge,
and I want that plunging.
I want the ones
who come in secret to drink
only in early darkness,
and I want the ones
who are swallowed.
I want the way
this water sees without eyes,
hears without ears,
shivers without will or fear
at the gentlest touch.
I want the way it
accepts the cold moonlight
and lets it pass,
the way it lets
all of it pass
without judgment or comment.
There is a lake,
Lalla Ded sang, no larger
than one seed of mustard,
that all things return to.
O heart, if you
will not, cannot, give me the lake,
then give me the song.

GIFT

R. S. Thomas

Some ask the world
    and are diminished
in the receiving
    of it. You gave me
only this small pool
    that the more I drink
from, the more overflows
    me with sourceless light.

110 POEMS OF LOVE AND REVELATION

THE HEAT OF MIDNIGHT TEARS
Mirabai

Listen, my friend, this road is the heart opening,
kissing his feet, resistance broken, tears all night.

If we could reach the Lord through immersion in water,
I would have asked to be born a fish in this life.
If we could reach Him through nothing but berries and wild
    nuts
then surely the saints would have been monkeys when they
    came from the womb!
If we could reach him by munching lettuce and dry leaves
then the goats would surely get to the Holy One before us!

If the worship of stone statues could bring us all the way,
I would have adored a granite mountain years ago.

Mirabai says, "The heat of midnight tears will bring you to God."

—Translated by Robert Bly

THE DOOR
Jane Hirshfield

A note waterfalls steadily
through us,
just below hearing.

Or this early light
streaming through dusty glass:
what enters, enters like that,
unstoppable gift.

And yet there is also the other,
the breath-space held between any call
and its answer—

In the querying
first scuff of footstep,
the wood owls' repeating,
the two-counting heart:

A little sabbath,
minnow whose brightness silvers past time.

The rest-note,
unwritten,
hinged between worlds,
that precedes change and allows it.

A Strange Feather

Hafiz

All
The craziness,
All the empty plots,
All the ghosts and fears,

All the grudges and sorrows have
Now
Passed.

I must have inhaled
A strange
Feather

That finally

Fell

Out.

—Translated by Daniel Ladinsky

THE MAN OF TAO
Chuang Tzu

The man in whom Tao
Acts without impediment
Harms no other being
By his actions
Yet he does not know himself
To be "kind," to be "gentle."

The man in whom Tao
Acts without impediment
Does not bother with his own interests
And does not despise
Others who do.
He does not struggle to make money
And does not make a virtue of poverty.
He goes his way
Without relying on others
And does not pride himself
On walking alone.
While he does not follow the crowd
He won't complain of those who do.
Rank and reward
Make no appeal to him;
Disgrace and shame
Do not deter him.
He is not always looking
For right and wrong
Always deciding "Yes" or "No."
The ancients said, therefore:
The man of Tao

Remains unknown
Perfect virtue
Produces nothing
'No-self'
Is 'True-Self.'
And the greatest man
Is Nobody."

—Translated by Thomas Merton

FIRE IN THE EARTH

David Whyte

And we know, when Moses was told,
   in the way he was told,
"Take off your shoes!" He grew pale from that simple

reminder of fire in the dusty earth.
   He never recovered
his complicated way of loving again

and was free to love in the same way
   he felt the fire licking at his heels loved him.
As if the lion earth could roar

and take him in one movement.
   Every step he took
from there was carefully placed.

Everything he said mattered as if he knew
   the constant witness of the ground
and remembered his own face in the dust

the moment before revelation.
   Since then thousands have felt
the same immobile tongue with which he tried to speak.

Like the moment you too saw, for the first time,
   your own house turned to ashes.
Everything consumed so the road could open again.

Your entire presence in your eyes
and the world turning slowly
into a single branch of flame.

THE DOVE DESCENDING
(FROM LITTLE GIDDING)

T. S. Eliot

The dove descending breaks the air
With flame of incandescent terror
Of which the tongues declare
The one discharge from sin and error.
The only hope, or else despair
  Lies in the choice of pyre or pyre—
  To be redeemed from fire by fire.

  Who then devised the torment? Love.
Love is the unfamiliar Name
Behind the hands that wove
The intolerable shirt of flame
Which human power cannot remove.
  We only live, only suspire
  Consumed by either fire or fire.

The Holy Longing

Johann Wolfgang von Goethe

Tell a wise person, or else keep silent,
Because the massman will mock it right away.
I praise what is truly alive,
What longs to be burned to death.

In the calm water of the love-nights,
Where you were begotten, where you have begotten,
A strange feeling comes over you
When you see the silent candle burning.

Now you are no longer caught
In the obsession with darkness,
And a desire for higher love-making
Sweeps you upward.

Distance does not make you falter,
Now, arriving in magic, flying,
And, finally, insane for the light,
You are the butterfly and you are gone.

And so long as you haven't experienced
This: to die and so to grow,
You are only a troubled guest
On the dark earth.

—Translated by Robert Bly

Prayer Is an Egg

Rumi

On Resurrection Day God will say, "What did you do with
the strength and energy

your food gave you on earth? How did you use your eyes?
What did you make with

your five senses while they were dimming and playing out?
I gave you hands and feet

as tools for preparing the ground for planting. Did you,
in the health I gave,

do the plowing?" You will not be able to stand when you
hear those questions. You

will bend double, and finally acknowledge the glory. God
will say, "Lift

your head and answer the questions." Your head will rise
a little, then slump

again. "Look at me! Tell what you've done." You try,
but you fall back flat

as a snake. "I want every detail. Say!" Eventually you
will be able to get to

a sitting position. "Be plain and clear. I have given you
such gifts. What did

you do with them?" You turn to the right looking to the
prophets for help, as

though to say, *I am stuck in the mud of my life. Help me
out of this!* They

will answer, those kings, "The time for helping is past.
The plow stands there in

the field. You should have used it." Then you turn to
the left, where your family

is, and they will say, "Don't look at us! This conversation
is between you and your

creator." Then you pray the prayer that is the essence
of every ritual: *God,*

*I have no hope. I am torn to shreds. You are my first and
last and only refuge.*

Don't do daily prayers like a bird pecking, moving its head
up and down. Prayer is an egg.

Hatch out the total helplessness inside.

—Translated by Coleman Barks

PRAYER
Carol Ann Duffy

Some days, although we cannot pray, a prayer
utters itself. So, a woman will lift
her head from the sieve of her hands and stare
at the minims sung by a tree, a sudden gift.

Some nights, although we are faithless, the truth
enters our hearts, that small familiar pain;
then a man will stand stock-still, hearing his youth
in the distant Latin chanting of a train.

Pray for us now. Grade I piano scales
console the lodger looking out across
a Midlands town. Then dusk, and someone calls
a child's name as though they named their loss.

Darkness outside. Inside, the radio's prayer—
Rockall. Malin. Dogger. Finisterre.*

*The poet is English, and these geographical markers are a well-known
feature of the local shipping forecast.

This Talking Rag

Hafiz

It
Was all
So clear this morning,

My mind and heart had never felt
More convinced:

There is only God,
A Great Wild
God.

But somehow I got yanked from
That annihilating
Realization

And can now appear again
As this wine-stained
Talking

Rag.

—Translated by Daniel Ladinsky

Maybe

Mary Oliver

Sweet Jesus, talking
  his melancholy madness,
    stood up in the boat
      and the sea lay down,

silky and sorry.
  So everybody was saved
    that night.
      But you know how it is

when something
  different crosses
    the threshold—the uncles
      mutter together,

the women walk away,
  the young brother begins
    to sharpen his knife.
      Nobody knows what the soul is.

It comes and goes
  like the wind over the water—
    sometimes, for days,
      you don't think of it.

Maybe, after the sermon,
  after the multitude was fed,
    one or two of them felt
      the soul slip forth

like a tremor of pure sunlight,
  before exhaustion,
    that wants to swallow everything,
      gripped their bones and left them

miserable and sleepy,
  as they are now, forgetting
    how the wind tore at the sails
      before he rose and talked to it—

tender and luminous and demanding
  as he always was—
    a thousand times more frightening
      than the killer sea.

DUST

Dorianne Laux

Someone spoke to me last night,
told me the truth. Just a few words,
but I recognized it.
I knew I should make myself get up,
write it down, but it was late,
and I was exhausted from working
all day in the garden, moving rocks.
Now, I remember only the flavor—
not like food, sweet or sharp.
More like a fine powder, like dust.
And I wasn't elated or frightened,
but simply rapt, aware.
That's how it is sometimes—
God comes to your window,
all bright light and black wings,
and you're just too tired to open it.

PERFECT JOY

Chuang Tzu

Here is how I sum it up:
   Heaven does nothing: its non-doing is its serenity.
   Earth does nothing: its non-doing is its rest.
   From the union of these two non-doings
   All actions proceed,
   All things are made.
   How vast, how invisible
   This coming-to-be!
   All things come from nowhere!
   How vast, how invisible
   No way to explain it!
   All beings in their perfection
   Are born of non-doing.
   Hence it is said:
   "Heaven and earth do nothing
   Yet there is nothing they do not do."

Where is the man who can attain
To this non-doing?

—Translated by Thomas Merton

LET'S GO HOME

Rumi

Late and starting to rain, it's time to go home.
We've wandered long enough in empty buildings.
I know it's tempting to stay and meet those new people.
I know it's even more sensible
to spend the night here with them,
but I want to go home.

We've seen enough beautiful places with signs on them
saying *This is God's house*.
That's seeing the grain like the ants do,
without the work of harvesting.
Let's leave grazing to cows and go
where we know what everyone really intends,
where we can walk around without clothes on.

—Translated by Coleman Barks

ABOUT THE POETS

FLEUR ADCOCK (b. 1937) was born in New Zealand and moved with her family to the United Kingdom when she was five, remaining there through World War II and until 1950, when the family went back to New Zealand. In 1963, after divorcing her first husband, she returned to Britain permanently with one of her two children, the other son remaining with his father in New Zealand. She became a professional librarian until 1980, except for a year when she went to live the life of a recluse in the English Lake District. It was during that year that she wrote the poem in this anthology. Since 1980 she has been a full-time writer, translator, and editor.

ANNA AKHMATOVA (1889-1966). The young Akhmatova knew French as well as the Russian poets by heart. She married the poet Nikolai Gumilyov in 1910 and for the next couple of years they traveled abroad, becoming friendly with Modigliani in Paris. Her first poetry collection, *Evening*, appeared in 1912. Two more marriages and several more collections followed, though after 1922 she had nothing else published until 1958, because her apolitical work was considered incompatible with the new order. Toward the end of her life, the ailing Akhmatova was acknowledged as the grande dame of Russian literature.

WENDELL BERRY (b. 1934), a farmer, lives in his native Kentucky. He is the author of more than thirty books of poetry, essays, and novels. His latest collection of poetry is *A Timbered Choir: The Sabbath Poems, 1979-1997*.

ROBERT BLY (b. 1926), poet, editor, translator, storyteller, and father of what he has called the "expressive men's movement," was born in Minnesota to parents of Norwegian stock. In 1956 he went to Norway on a Fulbright scholarship to translate Norwegian poetry into English, and returned to start a literary review, *The 50's*, then *The 60's* and *The*

70's, which introduced these poets to his generation. During the seventies he had eleven books of poetry, essays, and translations published, with four more appearing in the eighties. His most recent collection, of new and selected poems, is *Eating the Honey of Words*. His latest translations, of Ghalib, are in *The Lightning Should Have Fallen on Ghalib*.

CHUANG TZU (?-c. 275 B.C.) developed and articulated the teachings of the Taoist Lao Tzu, who died almost two hundred years before him. Chuang Tzu was the first to fully develop the Chinese Taoist teachings using parable, anecdote, allegory, and paradox. His work, known as The Chuang Tzu, was the foundation of what was to become the Taoist Way of Nature school of mystical philosophy.

BILLY COLLINS (b. 1941) is Professor of English at Lehman College, the City University of New York. He lives in Somers, New York. No poet since Robert Frost has managed to combine high critical acclaim with such broad popular appeal. The typical Collins poem opens on a clear and hospitable note but soon takes an unexpected turn. Poems that begin in irony may end in a moment of lyrical surprise. No wonder Collins sees his poetry as "a form of travel writing," and considers humor "a door into the serious." The author of seven volumes of poetry, his most recent work is *Nine Horses*, published in the fall of 2002. Collins is Poet Laureate of the United States, 2001-03.

E. E. CUMMINGS (1894-1962) was born in Cambridge, Massachusetts. In his poetry he experimented radically with form, punctuation, spelling, and syntax, creating a new, highly personal means of poetic expression. At the time of his death he was the second most widely read poet in the U.S. after Robert Frost.

EMILY DICKINSON (1830-86) lived her entire life as a recluse in Amherst, Massachusetts, though she actively maintained a wide correspondence and read exhaustively. Her work was heavily influenced by the Metaphysical poets of seventeenth-century England, as well as by her Puritan upbringing. Not publicly recognized during her lifetime, the first volume of her work was published posthumously in 1890, and the last in 1955.

CAROL ANN DUFFY (b. 1965), born in Glasgow, Scotland, is widely acclaimed as Britain's leading female poet. She studied philosophy at Liverpool University, and is currently poetry editor of *Ambit*. She also reviews new verse for *The Guardian* newspaper, and presents poetry on BBC radio. The most recent of her several collections of poetry are *Mean Time* (1993) and *The World's Wife* (1999).

T. S. ELIOT (1886-1965) was born in Missouri. In 1914, with degrees from Harvard, Eliot settled in England, marrying and working as a teacher, and later, in a bank and also as an editor at Faber and Faber. His first book of poems, *Prufrock and Other Observations*, was published in 1917, and immediately established him as the leading poet of the avant-garde. With the publication of *The Waste Land* in 1922, he became the dominant figure in poetry and literary criticism in the English speaking world. Many other major works followed, including *The Four Quartets* in 1943. He received the 1948 Nobel Prize in Literature.

RICK FIELDS (1942-99) was a well-loved and well-respected editor, author, and poet in the American Buddhist community. His several books on Buddhism include *Instructions to the Cook* (with Bernie Glassman) and *How the Swans Came to the Lake: A Narrative History of Buddhism in America*. Not long before he died, he published a limited edition of poems, *Fuck You, Cancer and Other Poems*.

ROBERT FROST (1874-1963) was born in San Francisco and grew up in Massachusetts. His father was a journalist, who died when Frost was eleven, and his Scottish mother resumed a schoolteaching career to support her family. He had a few poems published in the 1890s, worked many different jobs, from cobbler to Latin teacher, and married a former schoolmate, Elinor White. They had six children. In 1912 Frost took his family to England, and it was there that his first poetry collection, *A Boy's Will*, was published when he was thirty-nine. It was followed in 1914 by *North Boston*, which earned him an international reputation. Frost returned to the U.S. in 1915, bought a farm in New Hampshire, and taught at Amherst. His wife died in 1938, and he lost four of his children. Two of his daughters suffered mental breakdowns, and his son Carol committed suicide. Frost himself struggled with depression all his life. When he died, in 1963, he was the most popular and widely read poet in America.

MIRZA ASADULLAH KHAN GHALIB (1797-1869). Ghalib (a nom de plume that Mirza Khan adopted in the tradition of all classical Urdu poets of the time) was born in the city of Agra, in India. His father died when he was young and his mother's family raised him. At the age of thirteen, he was married and moved to Delhi, the Moghul capital. Ghalib matured intellectually at a very young age, and completed much of his great poetic output by the time he was nineteen. He was active in the spiritual and intellectual circles of Delhi, and his work shows a great knowledge of philosophy, ethics, theology, and classical literature. His *Diwan (Poetical Works)* is one of the treasures of Urdu literature, and was written at the time of the great renaissance of Urdu poetry, in the first half of the nineteenth century. In mid-life, Ghalib was employed as a teacher of poetry to the last Moghul emperor, yet even then, and throughout his life, his financial situation remained precarious. In his last years, under the rule of the British, Ghalib was in constant danger of being imprisoned, or worse, because of his ties with the Moghul aristocracy.

NIKKI GIOVANNI (b. 1943), a Black American poet, essayist, and lecturer, and native of Tennessee, now works as Professor of English at Virginia Polytechnic Institute. She has become a leading light of the Black Arts Movement, and an inspiration to Black women and writers. In the 1960s and '70s, her poetry strongly embraced the ideals of the Civil Rights and Black Arts Movements. Later, it explored her life as a single mother, and her personal relationships. Her collection *The Selected Poems of Nikki Giovanni* was published in 1996, and *Love Poems* in 1997.

JOHANN WOLFGANG VON GOETHE (1749-1832) was born in Frankfurt, Germany, into an upper-middle-class family, and began his studies at the age of sixteen at the University of Leipzig, where he wrote his earliest poems and plays. He then studied law in Strasbourg, and in 1775 was invited to the ducal court of Karl Augustus in Saxe-Weimar, where he held numerous high offices and spent most of the remainder of his life. During a two-year journey in Italy (1786-88) he recognized that he was an artist, and resolved to spend the rest of his life writing. Among his world-renowned works are *Faust, The Sorrows of Young Werther, Italian Journey,* and his scientific study, *Theory of Colors.* He died in Weimar at the age of eighty-two.

SHAMS-UD-DIN MUHAMMAD HAFIZ (c. 1320-89). Goethe was one of the first westerners to discover Hafiz (sometimes spelled Hafez), whom he considered "a poet for poets." Ralph Waldo Emerson discovered Hafiz through Goethe's work, and did several translations of his own into English. The complete collection of his poems, the *Diwan-i-Hafiz,* still sells more copies today in his native Persia (Iran) than any other book. Hafiz was born and lived in the city of Shiraz. Of lowly stock, he worked as a baker's assistant by day and put himself through school at night. Over many years he mastered the subjects of a classical medieval education, which included the great Persian poets. In medieval Persia poetry was valued very highly, and during his middle years, Hafiz served as a court poet. By the time he was sixty, he had become famous for his inspired verses, and he became both a spiritual and literary teacher for a wide circle of students. He was guided by a great Sufi master for most of his life, and he in his turn became a master for others in his later years.

SEAMUS HEANEY's (b. 1929) first published work, *Death of a Naturalist,* debuted in 1965. He has authored dozens more, including *Opened Ground* (1999), which was a *New York Times* Notable Book of the Year. He held the chair of Professor of Poetry at Oxford from 1989 to 1994, and in 1995 received the Nobel Prize in Literature. While he still lives in his native Northern Ireland, he has spent part of the year teaching at Harvard since 1981.

HILDEGARD OF BINGEN (1098-1179) was born to a noble German family, and when she was fourteen she chose the life of an anchorite (Christian hermit.) At the age of forty-three, she became the abbess of a community near Bingen, St. Rupert's Monastery. Over the course of ten years she wrote an account of her visionary experiences, which was published under the title *Scivias*. She is known to historians through her prodigious correspondence; to mystics for her book of visions; to medical historians and botanists for her two books on natural history and medicine; and to bishops, popes, abbots, and kings. Musicians have also discovered her antiphons, hymns, and a large body of mono-phonic chants, with text and music both by Hildegard. In her later life, she traveled extensively, preaching to religious and secular clergy.

JANE HIRSHFIELD (b. 1953) is a prize-winning poet, translator, edi-tor, and author of five collections of poetry. *Given Sugar, Given Salt* was a finalist for the National Book Critics Circle Award in 2001. Her work addresses the life of the passions, the way the objects and events of everyday life are informed by deeper wisdoms and by the darkness and losses of life. Her poetry searches continually for the point where new knowledge of the world and self may appear, and carries the influence of her lifelong study and practice of Buddhism. Originally from New York City, she has lived in the Bay Area for many years.

MARIE HOWE's (b. 1950) poems have appeared in *The New Yorker*, *The Atlantic, Harvard Review*, and *New England Review*, among others. She is the author of two collections of poetry, the most recent of which, *What the Living Do* (1998), is a result of her self-questioning and grief following the death of her brother from AIDS. Hers is a poetry of intimacy, witness, honesty, and relation. She teaches at Sarah Lawrence College.

JUAN RAMÓN JIMÉNEZ (1881-1958) was born in southern Spain, the son of a banker, and composed his first poems at the age of seven. In 1900 he was invited by the poet Rubén Darío to Madrid, where he became a member of the modernist literary circle and founded two literary reviews. When his father died later the same year, Jiménez fell into depression and returned to his birthplace. Poetry, the experience of beauty, became his means of struggling against an all-pervasive feeling of emptiness. Between the ages of twenty-four and thirty-one, he published nine volumes of poetry. He moved back to Madrid in 1912, and later, at the outbreak of the Spanish Civil War, he was made an honorary cultural attaché to the United States. He remained abroad from 1939 on, and in 1951 he settled with his wife in Puerto Rico, where he lectured at the university. In 1956 he received the Nobel Prize in Literature.

KABIR (1398-1448?), the son of a Muslim weaver, was born and lived in the Hindu holy city of Benares, India. A powerful spiritual teacher, he crossed the sectarian and religious divides of his day to attract both followers and enemies among Muslims and Hindus alike. He is widely thought to have been illiterate, and his poems—which were part of his teaching method—were given orally and written down by others. His central message was the necessity to see through our self-deceptions and recognize for ourselves the Truth that we are. Some of his couplets were preserved in the Adi Granth, the holy text of the Sikh religion, while the Bijak of Kabir contains only works attributed to him. The Bijak remains the scripture of the Kabir Panth, the monastic order that grew up around Kabir's teachings.

GALWAY KINNELL (b. 1927). Robert Langbaum, in *The American Poetry Review*, said of Kinnell that, "at a time when so many poets are content to be skillful and trivial, [he] speaks with a big voice about the whole of life." Throughout his work, Kinnell explores his relationship to transience, to death, the power of wilderness and wildness, and to the primitive underpinnings of existence. His is an intensely personal poetry, mining the depths of his own experiences of love, fatherhood, anxiety, and joy. He has been in residence at several universities, as well as a field worker for the Congress of Racial Equality. In 1983, he received the Pulitzer Prize for his *Selected Poems*.

STEVE KOWIT (b. 1938), a native of Brooklyn, was active in the poetry-reading coffeehouses of the Lower East Side during the 1960s. He studied poetry with Stanley Kunitz at New York City's 92nd Street Y and with Robert Lowell at the New School for Social Research. Author of a dozen collections since the sixties, Kowit's most recent volume of poetry, *The Dumbbell Nebula*, was published in 2000. He is also the editor of the anthology *Maverick Poets* and author of a guide to writing poetry, *In the Palm of Your Hand*. He now teaches at Southwestern College in Chula Vista, and lives in the San Diego backcountry.

STANLEY KUNITZ (b. 1905) worked for many years as an editor in New York City before achieving major recognition for his poetry, which came with a Pulitzer Prize in 1958 for his *Collected Poems*. Since then, he has won many prizes and honors. In 2000 he was the U.S. Poet Laureate, and in 1995 his collection *Passing Through* won the National Book Award. He taught for many years in the graduate writing program at Columbia, and continues to live in Manhattan and also in Provincetown, Massachusetts. His more recent poems combine a quiet restraint with a deep current of passion. Now well into his nineties, he continues to write actively.

PHILIP LARKIN (1922-85). After attending Oxford, Larkin's first book of poetry, *The North Ship*, was published in 1945. With the 1955 publication of his second volume, *The Less Deceived*, Larkin became the preeminent poet of his generation, and a leading voice of "The Movement," a group of young English writers who rejected the prevailing fashion for neo-romanticism. Larkin never married, and for the whole of his life led the quiet existence of a librarian in the northern English city of Hull.

DORIANNE LAUX (b. 1952) has an Irish, French, and Algonquin heritage, and grew up in Maine. Between the ages of eighteen and thirty she worked as a gas station manager, sanatorium cook, maid, and doughnut-holer. A single mother, she took occasional poetry classes at a local junior college, writing poems during shift breaks. In 1983 she moved to Berkeley, and began writing in earnest. Supported by scholarships and grants, she returned to school, and graduated in 1988 with a degree in English. Her first book of poems, *Awake*, was nominated for the San Francisco Bay Area Book Critics Award for Poetry. Her third collection, *Smoke*, was published in 2000.

D. H. LAWRENCE (1885-1930) was an acclaimed English novelist, short story writer, essayist, and poet. Though better known as a novelist, his first published works in 1909 were poems, and his poetry, especially his evocations of the natural world, have since had a significant influence on poets on both sides of the Atlantic. A writer with radical views, Lawrence regarded sex, the primitive subconscious, and nature as cures to what he saw to be the evils of modern industrial society. A lifelong sufferer of tuberculosis, he died in 1930 in France.

DENISE LEVERTOV's (1923-97) first book, *The Double Image*, which she wrote between the ages of seventeen and twenty-one, was published in 1946. Soon after emigrating from England to the United States, she was recognized as an important voice in the American avant-garde. Her next book, *With Eyes in the Back of Our Heads*, established her as one of the great American poets, and her English origins were forgotten. She published more than twenty volumes of poetry, and from 1989 to 1993 she taught at Stanford University. She spent the last decade of her life in Seattle, Washington. She was always an outsider, in England, in America, and also in poetry circles, for she never considered herself part of any school. She once said, "I nevertheless experienced the sense of difference as an honor, as part of knowing at an early age—perhaps by seven, certainly before I was ten—that I was an artist-person and had a destiny."

ANTONIO MACHADO (1875–1939) was a Spanish poet and school-teacher whose stature in the Spanish-speaking world is equal to Yeats and Rilke's in theirs. Born in Seville, he led a quiet though deeply passionate life. His poetry, too, has the quality of being both still and passionate at the same time. His words bring both gravity and luminosity to the simplest of events and objects. His first book, *Soledades*, published in 1903, includes the dream poem in this anthology. Besides poetry, Machado wrote newspaper articles on the political and moral issues of the time. In 1939, three years after the start of the civil war, he moved ahead of Franco's army and crossed the Pyrenees into France, dying of natural causes almost as soon as he arrived.

CZESLAW MILOSZ's (b. 1911) first work was published in 1933 in Poland, where his family moved from Lithuania soon after his birth. He joined the diplomatic service of People's Poland in 1945, and later sought asylum in France, where he wrote several works of prose. In 1953, he received the Prix Littéraire Européen, and in 1960 he moved to Berkeley, California, where he became Professor of Slavic Languages and Literature at the University of California. He has won many awards and prizes, culminating in the 1980 Nobel Prize in Literature. His most recent poetry collection is *New and Collected Poems, 1931-2001*. He writes poetry, Milosz says in *The Collected Poems 1931-87*, "to find my home in one sentence, concise, as if hammered in metal. Not to enchant anybody. Not to earn a lasting name in posterity. An unnamed need for order, for rhythm, for form, which three words are opposed to chaos and nothingness."

MIRABAI (1498-1550), born in Rajasthan, India, to a noble Rajput family, was married c. 1516 to the heir apparent of the ruler of Mewar. Her husband died before he could take the throne, and he left no heir. She left the court in her thirties, and became a wandering mendicant. She was a devotee of the god Krishna (whom she calls Giridhara "lifter of mountains") and dedicated all of her poems to him. She has remained immensely popular throughout India, and many English translations have been made of her poetry.

PABLO NERUDA (1904-73) is widely considered the most important Latin-American poet of the twentieth century, as well as an influential contributor to major developments in modern poetry. He was born in provincial Chile, the son of a teacher and a railway worker. He moved to the capital, Santiago, for his university education and published his first poetry collection, *Crepusculario*, in 1923 at the age of nineteen. *Twenty Love Poems and a Song of Despair*, which has since been translated into dozens of languages, came out the following year. Between 1927 and 1935 he held a series of honorary consulships around the world, returning to Chile in 1943 to become a senator of the Republic and a member of the Communist Party of Chile. His political interests strongly colored the poetic output of his middle years, though his complete oeuvre, running to several thousand pages, spans a vast range of ideas and passions. He received the 1971 Nobel Prize in Literature.

NAOMI SHIHAB NYE (b. 1952) was born of a Palestinian father and an American mother. Her work consistently reveals the poignancy and the paradoxes that emerge from feeling an intimate relationship with two different cultures. Raised in St. Louis, Missouri, she has lived in Jerusalem, and now resides with her family in San Antonio, Texas. Her poems and short stories have appeared in reviews and magazines all over the world. Besides her six volumes of poetry, she has also written books for children and edited several anthologies of prose. She first started writing poetry at the age of six. "Somehow, I knew what a poem was. I liked the comfortable, portable shape of poems . . . and especially the way they took you to a deeper, quieter place, almost immediately."

MARY OLIVER (b. 1935) is one of America's most widely read contemporary poets. The critic Alice Ostriker contends that Oliver is "as visionary as Emerson." She won her first poetry prize at the age of twenty-seven, from the Poetry Society of America, for her collection *No Voyage*. She won the Pulitzer Prize in 1984 for her collection of poems, *American Primitive*, and she was winner of the 1992 National Book Award for poetry for her *New and Selected Poems*. In an interview for the *Bloomsbury Review* in 1990, she said, "I feel that the function of the poet

110 POEMS OF LOVE AND REVELATION

is to be . . . somehow instructive and opinionated, useful even if only as a devil's advocate. . . . The question asked today is: What does it mean? Nobody says, 'How does it feel?'"

MARGE PIERCY (b. 1936), novelist, essayist, and poet, is best known for fiction with a feminist slant. Her writing stems from a political commitment that began with the Vietnam antiwar movement in the 1960s. She has published fourteen volumes of poetry. She edited the anthology *Early Ripening: American Women's Poetry Now* (1988) and is currently the poetry editor for *Tikkun* magazine. She lives with her husband, the writer Ira Wood, in Wellfleet, Massachusetts.

RAINER MARIA RILKE (1875-1926) survived a lonely and unhappy childhood in Prague to publish his first volume of poetry, *Leben und Lieder*, in 1894. In 1896 he left Prague for the University of Munich, and later made his first trip to Italy, and then to Russia. In 1902 in Paris he became friend and secretary to the sculptor Rodin, and the next twelve years in Paris were to see his greatest poetic activity. In 1919 he moved to Switzerland, where he wrote his last two works, *Sonnets to Orpheus* and *Duino Elegies*, in 1923. He died in Switzerland, of leukemia, in 1926. His reputation has grown enormously since his death, and he is now considered one of the greatest poets of the twentieth century.

RUMI (1207-73) was the founder of the Sufi order known as the Mevlevi (Whirling Dervishes) in Konya, Turkey. Though the theme of lover and beloved was already established in Sufi teaching, his own poetry was inspired by his meeting and the consequent loss of his great teacher, Shams of Tabriz. Out of their relationship was born some of the most inspired love poetry ever, in which Rumi sings of a love that is both personal and divine at the same time. After Shams's death, he would burst into ecstatic poetry anywhere, anytime, and his scribe and disciple, Husam, was charged with writing it all down. Rumi's great spiritual treatise, *The Mathnawi*, written in couplets, amounts to more than twenty-five thousand lines in six books.

EDITH SÖDERGRAN (1892-1923), born in St. Petersburg, Russia, spent most of her life in poor health and in isolation in southeast Finland, near the Russian border. *Dihter* (1916), her first book, was a collection of free verse that introduced the modernist movement to Finland and Sweden. *The Non-Existent Country* (1925) is among the most popular of her six volumes of poetry. She wrote in Swedish.

STEPHEN SPENDER (1909-95). From the time he was a student at Oxford, Spender led a glamorous and privileged life in the company of the literary and social luminaries of his day. Virginia Woolf and T. S. Eliot were his literary "parents" and champions, while W. H. Auden and Christopher Isherwood were lifelong friends and rivals. A humanist with deep socialist ideals, he fought in the Spanish Civil War, and during World War II he worked for the London Fire Service. He co-founded *Horizon* magazine with Cyril Connolly, and was editor of *Encounter* magazine, an English socialist intellectual review, from 1953 to 1966. He was Professor of English at University College, London, from 1970 to 1977, and was knighted in 1983. He published many volumes of poetry and essays, but his most famous work was his autobiography, *World Within World*, which gives an insider's perspective on the life of European intellectual and artistic circles of the first part of the twentieth century.

WILLIAM STAFFORD (1914-93), a native of Kansas, is a poet of ordinary life, and his collected poems are the journal of a man recording his daily experience of living. It was appropriate, then, that he would start every day at his writing desk. For Stafford, the smallest event and the smaller feelings that wash over us could be miracles. His poems are often short and unusually accessible, relying on the power of everyday speech to examine the world. His first major collection of poems, *Traveling Through the Dark*, was published when he was forty-eight, and won the National Book Award in 1963. He went on to publish more than sixty-five volumes of poetry and prose, and received many honors and awards. He was Consultant in Poetry to the Library of Congress, and taught for many years in Oregon.

ANNA SWIR (1900-84) was the only daughter of an impoverished painter, and grew up in his studio in Warsaw, Poland. A militant feminist and author of uninhibited love poems, her work conveys an erotic intensity and warmth, along with an empathy and compassion for those who suffer. Her poems on war and the Nazi occupation of Poland were among the finest of her generation. Czeslaw Milosz and Leonard Nathan have translated her work into English.

R. S. THOMAS (1913-2000) was the preeminent Welsh poet of the twentieth century. A fervent Welsh nationalist who learned the Welsh language, he nevertheless wrote all his poetry in English. Born in Cardiff and educated at the University College of North Wales, he was ordained as an Anglican priest in 1936, and spent his working life as a clergyman in rural Wales. He wrote about faith, nature, the Welsh countryside, and the landscapes within in more than twenty volumes of poetry. His *Collected Poems 1945-1990* was published in 1993. In 1964, he was awarded the Queen's Gold Medal for Poetry, and at the end of his life he was nominated for the Nobel Prize. His international standing rests primarily on the quality of his religious poetry.

DEREK WALCOTT (b. 1930) was born in St. Lucia, in the West Indies, and after attending university in Jamaica, moved to Trinidad to work as a theater and art critic. He financed his first publication, *25 Poems*, at the age of eighteen. Much of his work explores the tension of his dual African and European heritage. He has been a visiting professor at Harvard and other American universities, and now lives part of the year in the United States. He received the Nobel Prize in Literature in 1992 "for a poetic oeuvre of great luminosity, sustained by a historical vision, the outcome of a multicultural commitment."

DAVID WHYTE (b. 1955) was born and raised in the North of England, studied marine zoology in Wales, and trained as a naturalist in the Galapagos Islands. He now lives in the Pacific Northwest with his wife and two children, and works full time as a poet, reading and lecturing throughout the world. He is one of the few poets to bring his insights to bear on organizational life, working with corporations at home and abroad. He has published four volumes of poetry, and has also written two best-selling prose books.

WILLIAM WORDSWORTH (1770-1850) was born in the Lake District, in northern England, and his poetry is suffused with the rugged grandeur and beauty of that region. His mother died when he was eight, and his father died when he was still in school; the sense of being alone in the world is a theme that pervades his work, along with the love and kinship he felt for his sister. He studied at Cambridge, and before his final year, Wordsworth set out on a walking tour across Europe, which was to profoundly influence his poetic and also political sensibilities. The French Revolution aroused a strong interest in the life, troubles, and speech of the common man, all of which is evident in his poetry. His most famous work, *The Prelude*—a book-length autobiographical poem—is considered by many to be the crowning achievement of English romanticism. Though he worked on many versions of it through his lifetime, his wife, Mary, only finally published it posthumously, in 1850.

JAMES WRIGHT (1927-80) was born in Ohio, graduated from Kenyon College in 1952, and studied in Vienna the following year on a Fulbright Scholarship. In 1954 he went on to the University of Washington, where he studied with Stanley Kunitz and Theodore Roethke. *The Green Wall* was published in 1957, and he began to be published in every important journal from *The New Yorker* to *The New Orleans Poetry Review*. In the early sixties, Wright found a kindred spirit in Robert Bly; both of them were interested in a poetry that suggested there were vast powers that awaited release. Bly was the friend who was with Wright when he met the two horses described in his poem in this anthology, "The Blessing." He won many awards, including the Pulitzer, for his *Collected Poems*. He continued to write in a manner that was deliberately vulnerable, an extension of the "confessional" poetry current in the late fifties, yet transcending the merely personal to reach toward eternal and archetypal themes.

W. B. YEATS (1865-1939) was born into the Anglo-Irish landowning class in Dublin, the son of a well-known Irish painter, John Butler Yeats. He was educated in London and Dublin, and became involved in the Celtic Revival, a movement against the cultural influence of English rule. His writing at the turn of the century drew extensively from sources in Irish mythology and folklore. Another potent influence on his poetry was Maude Gonne, whom he met in 1889. Maude was equally famous for her passionate nationalist politics and her beauty. Though they both married other people, she remained a powerful figure in his poetry throughout his life. A lifelong fascination for mysticism and the occult is also strongly evident in his work. Elected a senator of the Irish Free Republic in 1922, Yeats is remembered today as one of the greatest poets of the twentieth century. He was awarded the 1923 Nobel Prize in Literature.

INDEX OF FIRST LINES

110 POEMS OF LOVE AND REVELATION

RISKING EVERYTHING

110 POEMS OF LOVE AND REVELATION

PERMISSIONS

Grateful acknowledgment is made to the following for permission to reprint previously published material:

Fleur Adcock, "Weathering" from *Poems 1960-2000*. Copyright © 2000 by Fleur Adcock. Reprinted with the permission of Bloodaxe Books Ltd.

Anna Akhmatova, "Everything Is Plundered" from *Poems of Akhmatova*, translated by Stanley Kunitz with Max Hayward (Houghton Mifflin). Copyright © 1973 by Stanley Kunitz and Max Hayward. Reprinted with the permission of Stanley Kunitz.

Wendell Berry, "The Peace of Wild Things" from *The Selected Poems of Wendell Berry*. Copyright © 1998 by Wendell Berry. Reprinted with the permission of Counterpoint Press, a member of Perseus Books, L.L.C. "A Homecoming" from *Country of Marriage* (New York: Harcourt Brace, 1973). Copyright © 1973 by Wendell Berry. Reprinted with the permission of the author.

Robert Bly, "People Like Us," "The Resemblance Between Your Life and a Dog," "Tasting Heaven," and "The Third Body" from *Eating the Honey of Words*. Copyright © 1999 by Robert Bly. "Things to Think" from *Morning Poems*. Copyright © 1997 by Robert Bly. All reprinted with the permission of HarperCollins Publishers, Inc.

Chuang Tzu, "When the Shoe Fits," "Perfect Joy," and "The Man of Tao," translated by Thomas Merton, from *The Way of Chuang Tzu*. Copyright © 1965 by The Abbey of Gethsemani. Reprinted with the permission of New Directions Publishing Corporation.

Billy Collins, "Shoveling Snow with Buddha" and "This Much I Do Remember" from *Picnic, Lightning*. Copyright © 1998 by Billy Collins. Reprinted with the permission of the University of Pittsburgh Press.

E. E. Cummings, "i thank You God for most this amazing" from *Complete Poems 1904-1962*, edited by George J. Firmage. Copyright 1950, © 1978, 1991 by the Trustees for the E. E. Cummings Trust. Copyright © 1979 by George James Firmage. Reprinted with the permission of Liveright Publishing Corporation.

Emily Dickinson, "Wild Nights" and "Soul *at the White Heat*" from *The Poems of Emily Dickinson*, edited by Thomas H. Johnson. Copyright © 1951, 1955, 1979 by the President and Fellows of Harvard College. Reprinted by permission of The Belknap Press of Harvard University Press and the Trustees of Amherst College.

Carol Ann Duffy, "Prayer" from *Mean Time*. Copyright © 1993 by Carol Ann Duffy. Reprinted with the permission of Anvil Press Poetry, Ltd.

T. S. Eliot, Part IV and Part V (excerpts) from "Little Gidding" from *Four Quartets*. Copyright 1943 by T. S. Eliot. Copyright renewed 1971 by Esme Valerie Eliot. Reprinted with the permission of Harcourt, Inc. and Faber & Faber, Ltd.

Rick Fields, "The Very Short Sutra on the Meeting of the Buddha and the Goddess" from *Dharma Gaia: A Harvest of Essays in Buddhism and Ecology*, edited by Allan Hunt-Badiner. Copyright © 1995 by Rick Fields. Reprinted with the permission of Marcia Fields.

Robert Frost, "The Road Not Taken" from *The Poetry of Robert Frost* edited by Edward Connery Lathem. Copyright 1916, © 1969 by Henry Holt and Company, copyright 1944 by Robert Frost. Reprinted with the permission of Henry Holt and Company, LLC.

Ghalib, "For the Raindrop." Copyright © 1989 by Jane Hirshfield. Reprinted with the permission of Jane Hirshfield.

Nikki Giovanni, "I Take Master Card (Charge Your Love to Me)" from *Love Poems*. Copyright © 1968, 1997 by Nikki Giovanni. Reprinted with the permission of HarperCollins Publishers, Inc.

Johann Wolfgang von Goethe, "The Holy Longing," translated by Robert Bly, from *The Soul Is Here for Its Own Joy: Sacred Poems from Many Cultures*, edited by Robert Bly (New York: The Ecco Press, 1995). Copyright © 1995 by Robert Bly. Reprinted with the permission of Robert Bly.

Hafez, "When the One I Love," translated by Robert Bly, from *The Soul Is Here for Its Own Joy: Sacred Poems from Many Cultures*, edited by Robert Bly. Copyright © 1995 by Robert Bly. Reprinted with the permission of Robert Bly. "A Strange Feather" and "This Talking Rag" from *The Gift: Poems by Hafiz, The Great Sufi Master*, translated by Daniel Ladinsky (New York: Penguin Compass, 1999). Copyright © 1999 by Daniel Ladinsky. Reprinted with the permission of the translator.

Seamus Heaney, "Postscript" from *The Spirit Level*. Copyright © 1996 by Seamus Heaney. Reprinted with the permission of Farrar, Straus & Giroux, LLC. and Faber & Faber, Ltd.

Hildegard of Bingen, "Holy Spirit," translated by Stephen Mitchell, from *The Enlightened Heart: An Anthology of Sacred Poetry*, edited by Stephen Mitchell. Copyright © 1989 by Stephen Mitchell. Reprinted with the permission of HarperCollins Publishers, Inc.

Jane Hirshfield, "The Door" and "Ripeness" from *The October Palace*. Copyright © 1994 by Jane Hirshfield. "Lake and Maple" and "Three Time My Life Has Opened" from *The Lives of the Heart*. Copyright © 1997 by Jane Hirshfield. All reprinted with the permission of HarperCollins Publishers, Inc.

Marie Howe, "My Dead Friends," "The Gate," and "The Promise" from *What the Living Do*. Copyright © 1997 by Marie Howe. Reprinted with the permission of W. W. Norton & Company, Inc.

Juan Ramón Jiménez, "Oceans" and "I Am Not I," translated by Robert Bly, from *The Soul Is Here for Its Own Joy: Sacred Poems from Many Cultures*, edited by Robert Bly (New York: The Ecco Press, 1995). Copyright © 1995 by Robert Bly. Reprinted with the permission of Robert Bly. "I Unpetalled You," translated by Stephen Mitchell, from *Into the Garden: A Wedding Anthology*, edited by Robert Hass and Stephen Mitchell. Copyright © 1993 by Stephen Mitchell. Reprinted with the permission of HarperCollins Publishers, Inc. "Life," translated by James Wright, from *Above the River: The Complete Poems*. Copyright © 1990 by Anne Wright. Reprinted with the permission of Wesleyan University Press.

Kabir, "A Place to Sit," "Breath," "The Unknown Flute," and "The Sound," translated by Robert Bly, from *The Soul Is Here for Its Own Joy: Sacred Poems from Many Cultures*, edited by Robert Bly (New York: The Ecco Press, 1995). Copyright © 1995 by Robert Bly. Reprinted with the permission of Robert Bly.

Galway Kinnell, "Rapture," "Parkinson's Disease," and "Oatmeal" from *A New Selected Poems*. Copyright © 1990, 1994 by Galway Kinnell. "The Cellist" from *Imperfect Thirst*. Copyright © 1994 by Galway Kinnell. Reprinted with the permission of Houghton Mifflin Company. All rights reserved.

Steve Kowit, "Notice" from *Mysteries of the Body*. Copyright © 1994 by Steve Kowit. Reprinted with the permission of the author.

Stanley Kunitz, "The Long Boat" from *Passing Through: The Later Poems New and Selected*. Copyright © 1985 by Stanley Kunitz. Reprinted with the permission of W. W. Norton & Company, Inc.

Philip Larkin, "Water" from *Collected Poems*, edited by Anthony Thwaite. Copyright © 1988, 1989 by the Estate of Philip Larkin. Reprinted with the permission of Farrar, Straus & Giroux, LLC and Faber & Faber, Ltd.

Dorianne Laux, "Dust" and "For the Sake of Strangers" from *What We Carry*. Copyright © 1994 by Dorianne Laux. Reprinted with the permission of BOA Editions, Ltd.

D. H. Lawrence, "Deeper Than Love" and "Snake" from *The Complete Poems of D. H. Lawrence*, edited by V. de Sola Pinto and F. W. Roberts. Copyright © 1964, 1971 by Angelo Ravagli and C. M. Weekley, Executors of The Estate of Frieda Lawrence Ravagli. Reprinted with the permission of Viking Penguin, a division of Penguin Putnam Inc.

Denise Levertov, "O Taste and See" from *Poems 1960–1967*. Copyright © 1964 by Denise Levertov. "That Day" and "Once Only" from *This Great Unknowing: Last Poems*. Copyright © 1998 by The Denise Levertov Literary Trust, Paul A. Lacey and Valerie Trueblood Rapport, Co-Trustees. All reprinted with the permission of New Directions Publishing Corporation.

Antonio Machado, "Last Night, As I Was Sleeping," "It's Possible," "The Wind, One Brilliant Day," and "Is My Soul Asleep?," translated by Robert Bly, from *Times Alone: Selected Poems of Antonio Machado*. Copyright © 1983 by Robert Bly. Reprinted with the permission of Robert Bly.

Czeslaw Milosz, "Encounter," "On Angels," "Gift," and "This Only" from *The Collected Poems, 1931-1987,* translated by Robert Hass. Copyright © 1988 by Czeslaw Milosz Royalties, Inc. Reprinted with the permission of HarperCollins Publishers, Inc. "Eyes" from *The New Yorker* (August 19 & 26, 2002). Copyright © 2002 by Czeslaw Milosz. Reprinted with the permission of the author.

Mirabai, "The Heat of Midnight Tears," and "All I Was Doing Was Breathing," translated by Robert Bly, from *Mirabai Versions.* Copyright © 1995 by Robert Bly. Reprinted with the permission of Robert Bly. "My Friends." Copyright © 1989 by Jane Hirshfield. Reprinted with the permission of Jane Hirshfield.

Pablo Neruda, "Ode to My Suit" from *Full Woman, Fleshly Apple, Hot Moon: Selected Poetry of Pablo Neruda,* translated by Stephen Mitchell. Copyright © 1997 by Stephen Mitchell. Reprinted with the permission of HarperCollins Publishers, Inc.

Pablo Neruda, "Poetry" translated by Alastair Reid, from *Selected Poems,* edited by Nathaniel Tarn. Copyright © 1970 by Anthony Kerrigan, W. S. Merwin, Alastair Reid, and Nathaniel Tarn. Reprinted with the permission of The Random House Group Limited.

Naomi Shihab Nye, "So Much Happiness" and "Kindness" from *Words Under the Words: Selected Poems* (Portland, Oregon: Far Corner Books, 1995). Copyright © 1995 by Naomi Shihab Nye. Reprinted with the permission of the author.

Mary Oliver, "When Death Comes" and "Maybe" from *New and Selected Poems.* Copyright © 1992 by Mary Oliver. Reprinted with the permission of Beacon Press, Boston. "Wild Geese" and "The Journey" from *Dream Work.* Copyright © 1986 by Mary Oliver. Reprinted with the permission of Grove/Atlantic, Inc. "In Blackwater Woods" from *American Primitive.* Copyright © 1983 by Mary Oliver. Reprinted with the permission of Little, Brown and Company (Inc.).

Marge Piercy, "To have without holding" from *The Moon Is Always Female.* Copyright © 1980 by Marge Piercy. Reprinted with the permission of Alfred A. Knopf, a division of Random House, Inc.

Rainer Maria Rilke, "Sometimes a Man Stands Up," "I Have Many Brothers," "Sunset," "You See, I Want a Lot," "The Swan," and "The Man Watching" from *Selected Poems of Rainer Maria Rilke,* translated by Robert Bly. Copyright © 1981 by Robert Bly. Reprinted with the permission of HarperCollins Publishers, Inc.

Rumi, "Today, Like Every Other Day" from *The Essential Rumi,* translated by Coleman Barks (New York: Harper, 1995). Copyright © 1995 by Coleman Barks. "Prayer Is an Egg," "Some Kiss We Want," and "Let's Go Home" from *The Soul of Rumi,* translated by Coleman Barks (San Francisco: HarperSanFrancisco, 2001). Copyright © 2001 by Coleman Barks. All reprinted with the permission of the translator.

Edith Södergran, "On Foot I Had to Walk Through the Solar Systems," translated by Stina Katchadourian from *Love and Solitude: Selected Poems 1916-1923.* Copyright © 1981, 1985, 1992. Reprinted with the permission of Fjord Press.

Stephen Spender, "I Think Continually of Those Who Were Truly Great" from *Collected Poems 1928-1985*. Copyright 1934 and renewed 1964 by Stephen Spender. Reprinted with the permission of Random House, Inc.

William Stafford, "Ask Me" from *The Way It Is: New and Selected Poems*. Copyright © 1977, 1998 by the Estate of William Stafford. Reprinted with the permission of Graywolf Press, St. Paul, Minnesota.

Anna Swir, "The Greatest Love," "Thank You, My Fate," and "The Same Inside," translated by Czeslaw Milosz and Leonard Nathan, from *Talking to My Body*. Copyright © 1996 by Czeslaw Milosz and Leonard Nathan. Reprinted with the permission of Copper Canyon Press, P.O. Box 271, Port Townsend, WA 98368-0271. "Dithyramb of a Happy Woman" from *Happy As a Dog's Tail*, translated by Czeslaw Milosz and Leonard Nathan (New York: Harcourt Brace, 1985). Copyright © 1985 by Czeslaw Milosz. Reprinted with the permission of the translators.

R. S. Thomas, "Gift" from *Collected Poems 1945-1990*. Copyright © 1993 by R. S. Thomas. Reprinted with the permission of The Orion Publishing Group.

Derek Walcott, "Love After Love" and "Oddjob, a Bull Terrier" from *Collected Poems 1948-1984*. Copyright © 1986 by Derek Walcott. Reprinted with the permission of Farrar, Straus & Giroux, LLC.

David Whyte, "Fire in the Earth," and "Sweet Darkness" from *Fire in the Earth*. Copyright © 1992 by David Whyte. "The Well of Grief" from *The House of Belonging*. Copyright © 1997 by David Whyte. Reprinted with kind permission of Many Rivers Press, Langley, WA. (360) 221-1324. www.davidwhyte.com.

James Wright, "A Blessing," "Milkweed," and "Today I Was Happy, So I Made This Poem" from *Above the River: The Complete Poems*. Copyright © 1990 by Anne Wright. Reprinted with the permission of Wesleyan University Press.

W. B. Yeats, "Vacillation, Part IV" from *The Collected Works of W. B. Yeats, Volume 1: The Poems, Revised*, edited by Richard J. Finneran. Copyright 1933 by The Macmillan Company, renewed © 1961 by Bertha Georgie Yeats. Reprinted with the permission of Scribner, an imprint of Simon & Schuster Adult Publishing Group.